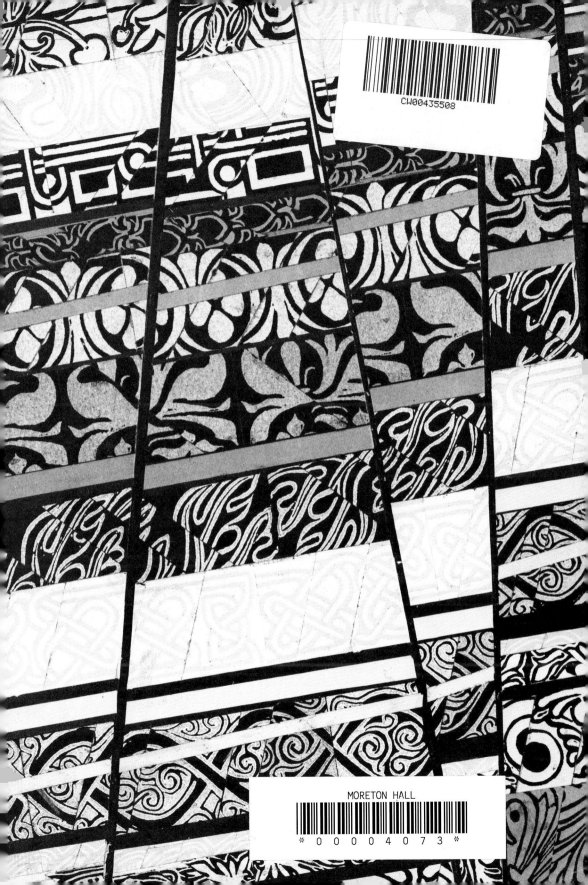

Alan Garner's
BOOK *of* BRITISH
FAIRY TALES

ALAN GARNER'S
BOOK *of* BRITISH
FAIRY TALES

Illustrations drawn and cut by Derek Collard

DELACORTE PRESS/NEW YORK

Published by
Delacorte Press
1 Dag Hammarskjold Plaza
New York, N.Y. 10017

This work was first published in Great Britain by William Collins
Sons & Co. Ltd.

Manufactured in Great Britain

First U.S.A. printing

Library of Congress Cataloging in Publication Data

Garner, Alan.
  Alan Garner's Book of British fairy tales.

  Bibliography: p.
  Summary: A collection of twenty-one traditional tales from the
British Isles.
    1. Fairy tales—Great Britain. [1. Fairy tales. 2. Folklore—Great
Britain] I. Collard, Derek, ill. II. Title. III. Title: Book of British
fairy tales.
PZ8.G226Bo   1985   398.2′0941
ISBN 0-385-29425-5
Library of Congress Catalog Card Number: 85-4586

CONTENTS

For John and Matthew

INTRODUCTION

Fairy tales were once for everybody, and it is a comparatively recent assumption that they are for children only. During the seventeenth and eighteenth centuries, in Britain, traditional stories of the fantastic and the supernatural came under attack: directly from the Church, for being either lies or the work of the Devil; indirectly from the educated and the literate, who followed the new sceptical materialism; and incidentally from the growth of towns and cities, which obliterated the oral traditions that a settled rural community may sustain, but an urban society of strangers does not. The result was that, by the middle of the nineteenth century, fairy tales that have existed in all times and in all places, as the common property of all, had been removed from their tellers and their audience and delivered up to child-minders and to scholars.

In the nursery, fairy tales became tracts to support authority, with moral lessons inserted and the wilder elements tamed so that children should not be exposed to unseemly events. And in the academic world, the duty of the folklorist was to rescue and record the stories that had survived, without concern for the popular audience. On the one hand, the texts were made literary and trite; and on the other, remote and unattractive, since the accurate transcription of spoken words carries with it little of the performance, in which the vitality lies.

By nature, fairy tale addresses itself to the ear rather than to the eye. Its first appeal is to a listener, and, since a listener is unable to stop and consider as a reader may, the form of the tale is direct. Plot evolves through physical action, and other concerns are kept in the listener's head by repetition. When literary styles, based on reason, try to make sense of fairy tale, they render it mundane; the meaning is in the music; it is in the language: not phonetics, grammar or syntax, but pitch and cadence, and the colour of the word.

In this selection of British fairy tales, I have tried to get back, through the written word, to a sense of the spoken. I have chosen stories that, though they may be shaped by literature in order to be read, are not descended from it. They are stories to be heard as well as seen. The purpose is not to record the moment of the telling, but to recreate the effect, so that, for the reader, the printed text may sing.

My concern for oral tradition goes back to my childhood, which was spent physically on the borders of suburbia, yet in a rural culture, as a member of a family long established in one place: Alderley Edge, a wooded hill in Cheshire.

Any disposition that there may have been for the telling of fairy tales had gone from that society before I was born; but there was a local legend, of a king asleep under the hill, which my grandfather made sure I knew, and in which he more than half believed. There was also a store of anecdote, accurately tied to place and people. Yet, during my childhood, I saw the end of both legend and anecdote as living things; the legend exists now only in print, and the anecdote only in notebooks and as a tape recorded archive. In that society now, the old are no longer a source of learning, and no one listens to what they could say. Defensively, they have stopped talking, and they make a virtue of dying with their knowledge unshared. Nothing comparable is replacing that knowledge, and the young inherit nothing of their own. Which is not to say that the expansion of sensibilities by modern techniques of communication is bad, but that, in the broadening of popular concerns, in the opening of the narrow societies to the world, much there that was good has been lost. A healthy future grows from its past; but today the links are being broken, both in the particular and in the general culture.

The loss of traditional fairy tales, and their replacement by more literary forms, is just such a debility. Fairy tales are now commonly tinkered with for biased ends; and they are subverted by knowing cynics, to be used as vehicles for private wit. Both are destructive acts of ignorance and of disaffection; and they are directed at children, who, lacking the rooted tradition, have only their instinct to keep them from the false.

The true fairy tale has no author. It derives from no source that we can identify, and from no known time. The irrational forces of which it is composed come from the depths of our humanity, and are universal. Here I have tried to show something of how those universal forces have expressed themselves in Britain; of how a people dreams.

Alan Garner.

TOM TIT TOT

ell, once upon a time, there was a woman and she baked five pies. And when they came out of the oven, they were that overbaked, the crust was too hard to eat. So she said to her daughter, "Put them pies on the shelf," she said, "and leave them a little, and they'll come again." She meant, you know, that the crust would get soft.

But the girl, she said to herself, "If they'll come again, I'll eat them now." And she set to work and ate them all, first and last.

Well, come supper time, the woman she said, "Go you and get one of them there pies. I daresay they've come again now."

The girl she went and she looked, and there wasn't nothing but the dishes. So back she came and said she, "No, they ain't come again."

"Not none of them?" said the mother.

"Not none of them," said she.

"Well, come again or not come again," said the woman, "I'll have one for supper."

"But you can't if they ain't come," said the girl.

"But I can," said she. "Go you and bring the best of them."

"Best or worst," said the girl, "I've ate them all, and you can't have one till it's come again."

Well, the woman she was wholly bate, and she took her spinning to the door, to spin, and as she spun she sang:

> "My daughter ate five, five pies today;
> My daughter ate five, five pies today."

The king was coming down the street, and he heard her sing, but what she sang he couldn't hear, so he stopped and said, "What was that you were singing of?"

The woman she was ashamed to let him hear what her daughter

had been doing, so she sang instead of that:

> "My daughter spun five, five skeins today;
> My daughter spun five, five skeins today."

"Stars of mine!" said the king. "I never heard tell of anyone who could do that."

Then he said, "Look you here, I want a wife, and I'll marry your daughter. But look you here," said he, "eleven months out of twelve she shall have all the vittles she likes to eat, and all the gowns she likes to get, and all the company she likes to keep; but the last month of the year she'll have to spin five skeins every day, and if she doesn't, I shall kill her."

"All right," said the woman; for she thought that was a grand marriage, that was. And as for them five skeins, when it came to, there'd be plenty of ways of getting out of it and likeliest he'd have forgotten about it.

Well, so they married. And for eleven months the girl had all the vittles she liked to eat, and all the gowns she liked to get, and all the company she liked to keep.

But when the time was getting over, she began to think about them there skeins, and to wonder if he had them in mind. But not one word did he say about them, and she wholly thought he'd forgotten.

However, the last day of the eleventh month, he took her to a room she'd never set eyes on before. There was nothing in it but a spinning wheel and a stool.

And said he, "Now, my dear, here you'll be shut in tomorrow, with some vittles and some flax, and if you haven't spun five skeins by the night, your head'll go off."

And away he went about his business.

Well, she was that frightened. She'd always been such a heedless girl that she didn't so much as know how to spin, and what was she to do tomorrow with no one to come near to help her? She sat down on a stool in the kitchen, and lork! how she did cry!

However, all on a sudden, she heard a sort of knocking low down on the door. She upped and opened it, and what should she see but a small little black thing with a long tail. It looked up at her right curious, and it said, "What are you crying for?"

"What's that to you?" said she.

"Never you mind," it said, "but tell me what you're crying for."

"It don't do me no good if I do," said she.

"You don't know that," it said, and twirled its tail round.

"Well," said she, "it won't do no harm, if it don't do no good," and she upped and told about the pies and the skeins and everything.

"This is what I'll do," said the little black thing. "I'll come to your window every morning, and take the flax and bring it spun at night."

"What's your pay?" said she.

It looked out of the corners of its eyes, and it said, "I'll give you three guesses every night to guess my name; and if you haven't guessed it before the month's up, you shall be mine."

Well, she thought she'd be sure to guess its name before the month was up. "All right," said she. "I agree."

"All right," it said, and lork! how it twirled its tail.

The next day her husband he took her into the room, and there was the flax and the day's vittles.

"Now there's the flax," said he. "And if that ain't spun up this night, off goes your head." And then he went out and locked the door.

He'd hardly gone, when there was a knocking against the window. She opened it, and there, sure enough, was the little old thing sitting on the ledge.

"Where's the flax?" it said.

"Here it be," said she. And she gave it to him.

Well, come the evening, a knocking fell again on the window. She opened it, and there was the little old thing, with five skeins of flax on its arm.

"Here it be," it said, and it gave the flax to the girl. "Now, what's my name?"

"What, is it Bill?" said she.

"No, it ain't," it said, and it twirled its tail.

"Is it Ned?" said she.

"No, it ain't," it said, and it twirled its tail.

"Is it Dick?" said she.

"No, it ain't," it said. And it twirled its tail harder, and away it flew.

Well, when the husband he came in, there were the five skeins ready for him.

"I see I shan't have to kill you tonight, my dear," said he. "You'll have your vittles, and your flax in the morning," said he, and away he went.

Well, every day the flax and the vittles, they were brought, and every day that there little black impet used to come mornings and evenings.

And all the day the girl she sat trying to think of names to say to it when it came at night, but she never hit on the right one. And as it got towards the end of the month, the impet it began to look so maliceful, and it twirled its tail faster and faster each time she gave a guess.

It came to the last day but one. The impet it came at night along with the five skeins, and it said, "What, ain't you got my name yet?"

"Is it Rob?" said she.

"No, it ain't," it said.

"Is it Hob?" said she.

"No, it ain't," it said.

"Is it Lob?" said she.

"No, it ain't that neither," it said.

Then it looked at her with its eyes like a coal of fire, and it said, "Woman, there's only tomorrow night, and then you'll be mine." And away it flew.

Well, she felt that horrid. However, she heard the king coming along the passage.

In he came, and when he saw the five skeins, he said, said he,

"Well, my dear, I don't see but what you'll have your skeins ready tomorrow night as well, and as I reckon I shan't have to kill you, I'll have supper in here tonight."

So they brought supper, and another stool for him, and down the two they sat.

Now he hadn't eaten but a mouthful or so, when he stopped and began to laugh.

"What is it?" said she.

"Why," said he, "I was out hunting today, and I got away to a place in the wood I'd never seen before. There was an old chalk pit. And I heard a sort of humming, kind of. So I got off my hobby, and I went right quiet to the pit, and I looked down. Well, what should there be but the funniest little black thing you ever set eyes on. And what was that doing but it had a little spinning wheel, and it was spinning wonderful fast, and twirling its tail. And as it spun, it sang:

> 'Nimmy nimmy not,
> My name's Tom Tit Tot!' "

Well, when the girl heard this, she fared as if she could have jumped out of her skin for joy; but she didn't say a word.

Next day, that there little thing looked so maliceful when it came for the flax. And at night, she heard it knocking against the window panes. She opened the window, and it came right in on the ledge. It was grinning from ear to ear, and oh! its tail was twirling round so fast.

"What's my name?" it said as it gave her the skeins.

"Is it Bullbeggar?" said she, pretending to be afraid.

"No, it ain't," it said, and it came further into the room.

"Is it Clabbernapper?" said she.

"No, it ain't," said the impet. And then it laughed and twirled its tail till you couldn't hardly see it. "Take time, woman," it said. "Next guess and you're mine!" And it stretched out its black hands to her.

She backed a step or two, and she looked at it, and then she laughed out, and said she, pointing of her finger at it:

"Nimmy nimmy not,
Your name's Tom Tit Tot!"

Well, when it heard her, it shruk awful, and away it flew, into the dark, and she never saw it no more.

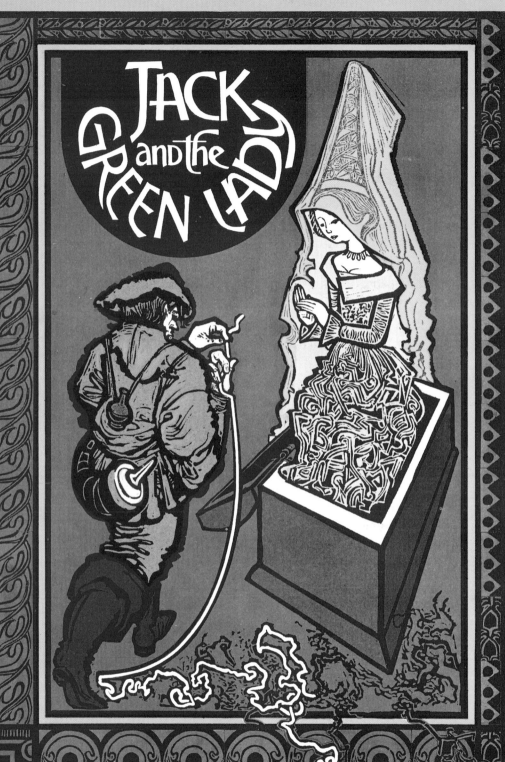

nce long ago, and a long time it was. If I were there then, I should not be there now. If I were there then and now, I should have a new story or an old story, or I should have no story at all.

However it was, Jack left home; and in the home, his old mother on a broken box.

He tramped along a dreary muddy road for miles and miles, and at last he took a seat and reconsidered himself; and he shook his head.

"Why did I, a foolish boy, leave my home?" said Jack. "Me, who was determined to see life, because I'd never seen life before! What is my old mother doing now without me?"

He shook his head again, but he plucked up courage, brushed his coat and his cap, and started on tramp once more. "Now, Jack," he said, as he sighed his way along the road, "there's only yourself you've got to talk to." He began to feel tired again, so he rested his weary foot. The night was dark, and bright stars above him, but he could not speak to the stars.

All at once, a clear light stood in front of him, so he glared at it at one side, and with his brain and his heart wondered and plundered what was going to be at the end. "Well, Jack old boy," he said, "cheer up; and now you must take some sleep."

At long last the morning came, and the birds began their bright singing, which lightened Jack a great deal. And the sun was shining so beautiful he could see the rocks and meadows clearly, and a large grey castle on a hill in front of him.

"Jack, my lad," he said, "you do not know what's before you; that castle may be your fortune."

He went on, and soon he sighed again; tired and dreary, hungry and thirsty, he glared at one side on a grey old farmhouse. He ventured to open the gate and knocked at the farm door, and asked the woman there for a drink. The old farmer woman asked him quite snubbily as she handed him the tea, "What is a young man like you doing about the country: have you no work?"

"No, there isn't no work for poor Jack," he said to the old farmer woman.

"Why?" she asked.

"Well," said Jack, "it's like a good few of you farmers; you're a bit superstitious of a man's stealing what you've got. But being as you made such a brag and a boast about it, we'll begin with you, missis. Is there any work for poor Jack from you?"

"Well, my man," she said, "only hard work."

Jack laughed as she stood with her coarse apron at the door. "Give me a chance, missis, to see what I can do."

"Well!" she said, quite sneery, "What can you do?"

"Excuse me," said Jack, quite on the laughing side, pulling his cap off so politely, and brushing back his black hair, "I'll give you an offer of work this instant minute. I'll chop that big tree for you, missis, into logs for your oven, for a bite to eat."

"Well," said the woman, "here's my chopper."

Jack smiled to himself and muttered, "She's a hard piece of brick is that farmer woman."

He worked away, did Jack, and, feeling very dreary, hungry and thirsty, brought the wood to the door.

"Jack," she said (quite the thing now), "you've done more work than any one of my men has done. Seat yourself down at the table, and eat and drink of the best."

"Now," Jack thought to himself, "it's only the start of a dream for you, my boy, it's only the first lesson. But somehow these hard-hearted manly women come soft-hearted at the end."

After he'd done his food, he sat himself down by the fireside and plundered very deeply about his poor old mother. And he started to make amends very smartly, and asked the woman could he have a wash.

"Of course," she said, quite cheerful; "it'll afresh you, Jack."

And out he went with the bucket and soap, and the farmer woman hurried after him, and delivered him the towel.

"Thank you kindly," said Jack. "You've been like a mother to me, but not exactly like my poor old mammy: she used to cling to me and pray for me more than anybody in the world."

Well, the woman fetched him a suit next, belonging to one of her sons, and begged him to stay the night. But all he said was, "How far is the next village from here, missis?"

"You don't mean to say you will walk twenty miles tonight, Jack," she said. "I want you to stay with me, and I'll give you good money, and good food. Do you know owt about ploughing?"

"No," he said, quite stern to the woman. "The best ploughing I ever did is ploughing the hard road. So I'll stay no longer than tonight, and mind you call me up at six o'clock in the morning."

The next morning came. He heard the gentle creak on the stairs, and up he jumped on the cheerful side. "Well, Jack," he said to himself, "you do look a smart, brisk lad now. And you'll soon make away for your dear hard road."

He enjoyed his breakfast with the woman, and told her straight he must leave that same morning.

"Poor foolish Jack!" she said, with a jeery laugh. "I suppose you're thinking of that grey castle. There's nowt there for you, my boy, nowt whatsoever! The very idea of you going there! Poor foolish lad!"

"Well," said Jack, "I'm determined to see life; and life I will see."

So off he went, carrying a little food with him. He shut the gate behind him merrily, and started laughing. "Oh," he said, "I'm on the hard road again!"

He started a bit of fast walking, for he gave no thought for those twenty miles, and he walked and walked till he saw the castle grinning at him. He sat himself down and he smiled to himself. "I'll soon make that castle speak," he said. "It's been on my brain long enough."

He could see the lodge of the castle, but no light in the lodge.

However, when he got to the door he saw a light inside, so he smartened himself and gave a knock on the hard knocker. An old grey lady came out to him. She opened the door and gave him a little smile.

"What can you want here, boy?" she said.

"What a different voice she has from that hard brick," Jack said to himself. And he laughed. "I want to know, mother," he said out loud, "who lives up at that grey castle."

"You come in, boy, and I'll try to explain to you," she said. "You're very late. Are you looking for work? I've been here these thirty years, and I've seen no man like you walking about the land. But there's no harm in you going up. There's only an old gentleman there, and he's deaf."

"Ah," said Jack. "Never enter, never will. And I'm going up, mother."

"Good night, boy," she said. "Take care of yourself: you've got two miles yet to go up to the castle."

Jack went along through two big iron gates, and made his way to the castle. He went over old humpy, old bumpy, old stones, but he didn't care for the humpy bumpy stones. He came to the door of the castle: dirty big lumps of lead on that door, but a beautiful knocker. He knocked at the door.

The door opened, but he saw no one there. He could not understand it. The door closed again. He knocked again. The door opened again. But still he saw no one there.

Jack stepped in then, cheekily. And what stood before him? A little hairy old man.

"What can I do for you?" said the hairy man.

"I want work, sir," said Jack.

"Ha! ha! ha!" said the hairy man. "Work you want, is it? Come this way. I'll show you work! Did anyone send you up here?"

"No," said Jack, quite cheerful.

"You're brave," said the hairy man. "There hasn't been anyone up here for thirty years. Well," he said, "I'll see about getting some work for you. When did you eat today?"

"Oh, I don't feel hungry," said Jack.

"Well, I do," said the hairy man. "Come this way. You have not seen the master yet."

Jack began to shiver. Jack began to stare. And who should sit down at the great dinner table but a big giant! Jack stared and stared.

"Well, my brave man," said the giant, "come to look for work, have you? Ha! Ha! I'll give you work, if work it is you want!"

Jack began to miss the little hairy man.

"Sit down there," said the giant.

Jack saw an enormous plate before him.

"You've to eat all that!" said the giant. "Remember you haven't seen your master yet."

"How many masters must I see?" Jack said to himself. But he ate the plateful of food.

"You'll want a place to sleep in, won't you?" said the giant.

"Yes," said Jack.

"Come here and I'll show you."

And there stood Jack's dear little hairy man. Jack stepped after him into a room and saw a huge bed. "Too big for me," said Jack to himself.

Then who dropped in but a bigger giant than the first, and one that would have been the mainstay of two giants!

"You're not sleeping with me?" said Jack.

"No, my man," said the giant. "That is your bed to yourself."

"I'll be glad of a rest," said Jack. And he pulled his shoes off, and he put his head down on the pillow, and he snored and snored till morning. You would hardly know that it was morning there; it was always so dark.

A ten-pound knock came at the door and shook Jack's bed from under him.

"Come down to your breakfast, my man, come down!" said the giant.

Poor Jack went down for his breakfast; certainly he did. And he saw the two giants and the little shrimp, the hairy man.

"Jack," said the first giant, "I want you to do some very hard work today. You're to go into the green room today. There stands a table before you, my boy, and you'll have to sleep there for three nights, my boy, and unpick every single bit of rag that's in that great big rug."

"I'll try my best, sir," said Jack, shivering again. The giant went away and slammed the door on him.

There were only two candles for his work. (He must have had good eyes, too.) So he picked up the rug and started working. At last he began to tremble: he partly knew there was somebody about. And the enormous big giant with his glistening eyes came in.

"Well, Jack," he said, "have you found anything? Have you seen anything?"

"What do you want me to see or find?" said Jack. "Is there anything in this dark room to find or to see?"

"Seek not for information," said the big giant, "but get on with your work!" The door went slam, with a fast lock.

Jack began to work again, and he looked towards a big long chest that stood in the darkest corner. He heard a whisper in the chest: "Unpick the rug from the middle, Jack, and your three days' task will soon be finished. But do not say that you heard anything."

The big giant came in, shining the room up with his glittering eyes. "You're doing your work wonderful, Jack," he said, "but I'm not quite satisfied. You must have seen someone to help you do that rug."

"I don't know what you are talking about," said Jack.

The giant went out the same old way with a slam of the door.

It struck Jack about the old chest that stood in the corner. He stepped up to it and was tempted to undo the lock. The word was spoken: "You can't undo that lock. Look on the shelf, Jack, and look pretty sharp, and you'll find the key of the chest." Jack looked sharp, and found the key.

He unlocked the chest, and the lid opened, and he staggered back.

22

He saw inside the sparkle of a beautiful green dress, and a pale face: a lovely lady. Then she up and spoke to Jack before she lay down again. "Jack," she said, "I have been locked in this chest for the last thirty years." Jack was staggered. "Are you a ghost?" he said.

"No," she said. "I'm human like you are; there's still a bit of life in me. I'm in my wedding dress. You are my brave man, Jack. Those two giants are enchanted, and that little hairy man is my father. And now, Jack, I've told you my secret. So don't hesitate, Jack; close the chest, fasten the lock, and say nothing."

By this time the whole rug is unpicked.

At last bum! bum! bum! the giant came. "Come in!" said Jack.

"My word!" said the giant. "You have worked that cloth beautiful, Jack. You must have found something, or seen someone. There's only one more thing, Jack, you've got to do for me: to go to that pond outside the castle and find two diamond rings."

"Well," said Jack, "that's impossible, sir, to find two diamond rings."

The giant glared at him quite furiously.

Poor Jack went out to the dirty black pond, and he plundered to himself could he find these two diamond rings. He saw a white swan, and he thought to have a chat with this swan, but it reared up at him, and Jack got more frightened of the swan than he was of the two giants.

"Jack," said the swan, "follow me, and I'll show you where are those diamond rings."

Jack followed the swan up to the pond.

"Don't get disheartened, Jack," she said. "I've got those diamond rings for you." And the swan lifted up her bill, and there were the rings she had picked up from the bottom of the pond. "And now, Jack," she said, "go back to that giant, and tell him you've seen no one, and give those two rings into his hands."

Back went Jack, quite cheerful, stepped into the green room, went up to the chest the first thing, and opened the lid, and spoke gently to the lovely green lady. He showed her the rings.

"Jack," she said, "my good lad, give them to that brute, and do not return here again to me. You will find me somewhere else."

Jack went bravely from her, and stepped up to the big giant. "Here you are, brute," he said.

"What!" said the giant. "Those same two diamond rings that caused a lot of bloodshed? Well, Jack, you've fulfilled your work; you've beaten me, Jack. And you've won the grey castle. You'll be poor Jack no longer. Go into the green room, and you shall have your reward."

Jack went into the other room quite happy and proud, and a nice gentleman met him at the door. He was looking for the little hairy man, but he couldn't see him: only this very nice gentleman to keep poor Jack company.

Then he saw the castle all of a light-shine, which he had never seen before. The gentleman danced him into another great room, and he could see the table laid out with chickens and ducks and all sorts of good things, and he was plundering where were the guests. And two young men appeared, shining like the rising sun. He was looking for the two giants, and lo and behold! – these two gentlemen.

Jack was quite excited and quite exhausted. Then who came in after, but a lovely lady in a pale green dress and a green veil. She came up to Jack and said, "Jack, my boy, you have broken our enchantment!" With that, she threw back her green veil, and stood before him, the most handsome young lady in all the land.

Then they all gathered together – the father, the two brothers, and Jack and the lady – without one enemy in the world. And Jack married the lovely lady. And so they lived happy for ever more after.

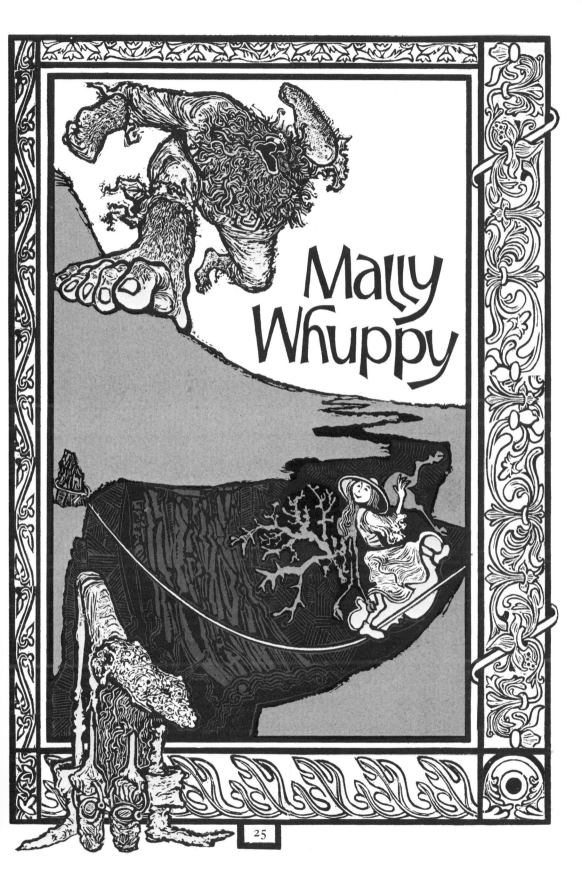

Mally Whuppy

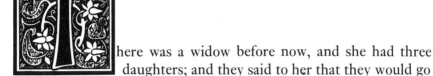here was a widow before now, and she had three daughters; and they said to her that they would go to seek their fortunes. She baked three bannocks, and said to the big daughter, "Which would you like best: the little half and my blessing, or the great half and my curse?"

"I like best," said the daughter, "the great half and your curse."

She said to the middle daughter, "Which would you like best: the little half and my blessing, or the great half and my curse?"

"I like best," said the daughter, "the great half and your curse."

She said to the small daughter, "Mally Whuppy, which would you like best: the little half and my blessing, or the great half and my curse?"

Mally Whuppy, the small daughter, said, "I like best the little half and your blessing."

This pleased the mother, and she gave Mally Whuppy the two other halves also.

The daughters went away, but the two eldest did not want the youngest to be with them, and they tied her to a rock of stone. They went on; but her mother's blessing came and freed her, and when they looked behind them they saw Mally Whuppy coming, with the rock on top of her.

They let her alone a turn of a while, till they reached a peat stack, then they tied her to the stack. They went on a bit; but her mother's blessing came and freed her, and when they looked behind them they saw Mally Whuppy coming with the peat stack on top of her.

They let her alone a turn of a while, till they reached a tree, and then they tied her to the tree. They went on a bit; but her mother's blessing came and freed her, and when they looked behind them they saw Mally Whuppy coming with the tree on top of her.

They saw it was no good to be at her, so they loosed her and let her go with them.

They went till night was on them, and they came to a giant's house. They asked to stop the night. They got that, and they were put to bed with the three daughters of the giant.

There were twists of amber knobs about the necks of the giant's daughters, and strings of horse hair about their own. They slept, but Mally Whuppy did not sleep.

Through the night a thirst came on the giant. He called to his bald, rough-skinned gillie to bring him water. "There is not a drop within," said the bald, rough-skinned gillie.

"Kill," said the giant, "one of the strangers, and fetch me her blood."

"How will I know them?" said the bald, rough-skinned gillie.

"There are twists of knobs of amber about the necks of my daughters," said the giant, "and twists of horse hair about the necks of the rest."

Mally Whuppy heard the giant, and as quick as she could she put the strings of horse hair that were about her own neck and about the necks of her sisters about the necks of the giant's daughters; and the knobs of amber that were about the necks of the giant's daughters about her own neck and about the necks of her sisters; and she lay down so quietly.

The bald, rough-skinned gillie came and felt at the necks, and he killed one of the giant's daughters, and took the blood with him. The giant said, "Fetch me more." The bald, rough-skinned gillie killed another. The giant said, "Fetch me more," again. Then the bald, rough-skinned gillie killed the last.

Mally Whuppy awoke her sisters, and she took them with her on top of her, and out she went.

The giant perceived her, and he followed.

The sparks of fire that she kindled from the stones with her heels were striking the giant on the chin; and the sparks of fire that the giant was bringing out of the stones with the points of his feet, they were striking Mally Whuppy in the back of the head. And so they

27

went until they reached a river.

Mally Whuppy plucked a hair out of her head and made a bridge of it, and she ran over the river, and the giant could not cross.

"You are over there, Mally Whuppy," said the giant.

"I am, though it is hard for thee."

"You killed my three bald brown daughters."

"I killed, though it is hard for thee."

"When will you come again?"

"I shall come when my business brings me."

Mally Whuppy went on forward till she reached the house of a farmer. The farmer had three sons. Said the farmer to Mally Whuppy, "I will give my big son to your big sister, and you get for me the fine comb of gold and the coarse comb of silver that the giant has."

"It will cost you no more," said Mally Whuppy.

She went back to the house of the giant, and got in unknown. She took with her the fine comb of gold and the coarse comb of silver, and out she went. The giant perceived her, and he followed till they reached the river. She crossed by the bridge of one hair, and the giant could not cross.

"You are over there, Mally Whuppy," said the giant.

"I am, though it is hard for thee."

"You killed my three bald brown daughters."

"I killed, though it is hard for thee."

"You stole my fine comb of gold and my coarse comb of silver."

"I stole, though it is hard for thee."

"When will you come again?"

"I shall come when my business brings me."

She gave the combs to the farmer, and her big sister and the farmer's big son were married.

"I will give my middle son to your middle sister," said the farmer, "and you get for me the giant's best buck."

"It will cost you no more," said Mally Whuppy.

She went back to the house of the giant, and hid by the well. In the night, the bald, rough-skinned gillie came out to draw water, and when he bent his back Mally Whuppy pushed him into the well and drowned him. Then she took the giant's best buck, and off she went. The giant perceived her, and he followed till they reached the river. She crossed by the bridge of one hair, and the giant could not cross.

"You are over there, Mally Whuppy," said the giant.

"I am, though it is hard for thee."

"You killed my three bald brown daughters."

"I killed, though it is hard for thee."

"You stole my fine comb of gold and my coarse comb of silver."

"I stole, though it is hard for thee."

"You killed my bald, rough-skinned gillie."

"I killed, though it is hard for thee."

"You stole my best buck."

"I stole, though it is hard for thee."

"When will you come again?"

"I shall come when my business brings me."

She gave the buck to the farmer, and her middle sister and the farmer's middle son were married.

"I will give you my youngest son," said the farmer, "and you bring me the golden bedspread the giant has."

"It will cost you no more," said Mally Whuppy.

She went back to the house of the giant, and got in unknown; but when she had hold of the bedspread the giant awoke and caught her.

"What, Mally Whuppy," said the giant, "would you do to me, if I had done as much harm to you as you have done to me?"

"I should put you in a sack," said Mally Whuppy, "hang the sack from the roof-tree, and set fire under you, and pound you with clubs till you fell on the floor."

"That same," said the giant, "I shall do to you." And he put her in a sack and hung her from the roof-tree, and went out to fetch wood for the fire.

When the giant was gone, Mally Whuppy began to shout, "I am in the light! I am in the light! I am in the city of gold!"

The giant's mother heard her and came running.

"I am in the light!" cried Mally Whuppy.

"Will you let me in?" said the carlin.

"I will not," said Mally Whuppy.

The carlin set down the sack. "Will you let me in?" she said again.

"Oh, very well," said Mally Whuppy, and she came out of the sack and let the giant's mother get in.

Then Mally Whuppy put in a cat, and a calf and a cream dish on top of the carlin, took up the golden bedspread, and went away.

The giant came in with the wood, and lit a fire beneath the sack and began to pound the sack with clubs.

"It's me in here! It's me in here!" shouted his mother.

"I know it's you in there," said the giant, and pounded the harder. And what with the din from the cat, the calf, the carlin and the cream dish, he thought he had done for Mally Whuppy. He opened the sack, and found his mother in it.

When the giant saw how it was, he followed Mally Whuppy till she crossed the river by the bridge of one hair, and the giant could not cross.

"You are over there, Mally Whuppy," said the giant.

"I am, though it is hard for thee."

"You killed my bald brown daughters."

"I killed, though it is hard for thee."

"You stole my fine comb of gold and my coarse comb of silver."

"I stole, though it is hard for thee."

"You killed my bald, rough-skinned gillie."

"I killed, though it is hard for thee."

"You stole my best buck."

"I stole, though it is hard for thee."

"You killed my little grey mother."

"I killed, though it is hard for thee."

"You stole my golden bedspread."

"I stole, though it is hard for thee."

"When will you come again?"

Mally Whuppy

"I shall come when my business brings me."

"Mally Whuppy," said the giant, "if you were over here, and I yonder, what would you do to follow me?"

Mally Whuppy said, "I should stick myself down, and I should drink till I should dry the river."

The giant stuck himself down, and he drank till he burst. And Mally Whuppy went and gave the golden bedspread to the farmer; and she was married to his youngest son that night.

YALLERY BROWN

've heard tell as how the bogles and boggarts were main bad in the old times, but I can't rightly say as I ever saw any of them myself, not rightly bogles, that is, but I'll tell you about Yallery Brown. If he wasn't a boggart, he was main near it, and I knew him myself. So it's all true – strange and true I tell you.

I was working on the High Farm to then, and nobbut a lad of sixteen or maybe eighteen years; and my mother and folks dwelt down by the pond yonder, at the far end of the village.

I had the stables and such to see to, and the horses to help with, and odd jobs to do, and the work was hard, but the pay good. I reckon I was an idle scamp, for I couldn't abide hard work, and I looked forward all the week to Sundays, when I'd walk down home, and not go back till darklins.

By the green lane I could get to the farm in a matter of twenty minutes, but there used to be a path across the west field yonder, by the side of the spinney, and on past the fox cover, and I used to go that way. It was longer for one thing, and I wasn't never in a hurry to go back to work, and it was still and pleasant like of summer nights, out in the broad silent fields, mid the smell of the growing things.

Folk said as the spinney was haunted, and for sure I have seen lots of fairy stones and rings and that, along the grass edge; but I never saw nowt in the way of horrors and boggarts, let alone Yallery Brown, as I said before.

One Sunday, I was walking across the west field. It was a beautiful July night, warm and still, and the air was full of little sounds, as if the trees and grass were chattering to their selves. And all to once there came a bit ahead of me the pitifullest greeting I've ever heard, sob, sobbing, like a bairn spent with fear, and near heart-broken; breaking off into a moan, and then rising again in a long, whimpering

33

wailing that made me feel sick nobbut to hark to it. I was always fond of babbies, too, and I began to look everywhere for the poor creature.

"Must be Sally Bratton's," I thought to myself. "She was always a flighty thing, and never looked after it. Like as not, she's flaunting about the lanes, and has clean forgot the babby."

But though I looked and looked I could find nowt. Nonetheless the sobbing was at my very ear, so tired like and sorrowful that I kept crying out, "Whisht, bairn, whisht! I'll take you back to your mother if you'll only hush your greeting."

But for all my looking I could find nowt. I keekit under the hedge by the spinney side, and I clumb over it, and I sought up and down by, and mid the trees, and through the long grass and weeds, but I only frightened some sleeping birds, and stinged my own hands with the nettles. I found nowt, and I fair gave up to last; so I stood there, scratching my head, and clean beat with it all. And presently the whimpering got louder and stronger in the quietness, and I thought I could make out words of some sort.

I harkened with all my ears, and the sorry thing was saying all mixed up with sobbing:

"O, oh! The stone, the great big stone! O, oh! The stone on top!"

Naturally I wondered where the stone might be, and I looked again, and there by the hedge bottom was a great flat stone, near buried in the mools, and hid in the cotted grass and weeds. One of those stones as were used to call the Strangers' Tables. The Strangers danced on them at moonlight nights, and so they were never meddled with. It's ill luck, you know, to cross the Tiddy People.

However, down I fell on my knee-bones by the stone, and harkened again. Clearer nor ever, but tired and spent with greeting, came the little sobbing voice.

"Ooh! Ooh! The stone, the stone on top!"

I was misliking to meddle with the thing, but I couldn't stand the whimpering babby, and I tore like mad at the stone, till I felt it lifting from the mools, and all to once it came with a sigh, out of the damp earth and the tangled grass and growing things. And there, in the hole, lay a tiddy thing on its back, blinking up at the moon and at me.

It was no bigger than a year-old brat, but it had long cotted hair and beard, twisted round and round its body, so as I couldn't see its clouts. And the hair was all yaller and shining and silky, like a bairn's; but the face of it was old, as if it were hundreds of years since it was young and smooth. Just a heap of wrinkles, and two bright black eyes in the mid, set in a lot of shining yaller hair; and the skin was the colour of the fresh turned earth in the Spring – brown as brown could be, and its bare hands and feet were brown like the face of it.

The greetin had stopped, but the tears were standing on its cheek, and the tiddy thing looked mazed like in the moonshine and the night air. I was wondering what I'd do, but by and by it scrambled out of the hole, and stood looking about it, and at myself. It wasn't up to my knee, but it was the queerest creature I ever set eyes on. Brown and yaller all over; yaller and brown, as I told you before, and with such a glint in its eyes, and such a wizened face, that I felt feared on it, for all that it was so tiddy and old.

The creature's eyes got some used to the moonlight, and presently it looked up in my face as bold as ever was.

"Tom," it says, "you're a good lad."

As cool as you can think, it says, "Tom, you're a good lad," and its voice was soft and high and piping like a little bird twittering.

I touched my hat, and began to think what I ought to say; but I was clemmed with fright, and I couldn't open my gob.

"Houts!" says the thing again. "You needn't be feared of me; you've done me a better turn than you know, my lad, and I'll do as much for you."

I couldn't speak yet, but I thought: "Lord! For sure it's a bogle!"

"No!" it says, quick as quick, "I'm not a bogle, but you'd best not ask me what I am; anyways, I'm a good friend of yours."

My very knee-bones struck, for certainly an ordinary body couldn't have known what I'd been thinking to myself, but it looked

35

so kind like, and spoke so fair, that I made bold to get out, a bit quavery like:

"Might I be asking to know your honour's name?"

"Hm," it says, pulling its beard, "as for that," and it thought a bit, "ay so," it went on at last, "Yallery Brown you may call me; Yallery Brown. It's my nature, you see. And as for a name, it will do as well as any other. Yallery Brown, Tom, Yallery Brown's your friend, my lad."

"Thank you, master," says I, quite meek like.

"And now," he says, "I'm in a hurry tonight, but tell me quick, what shall I do for you? Will you have a wife? I can give you the rampingest lass in the town. Will you be rich? I'll give you gold as much as you can carry. Or will you have help with your work? Only say the word."

I scratched my head. "Well, as for a wife, I have no hankering after such. They're but bothersome bodies, and I have women folk at home as will mend my clouts. And for gold; that's as may be," for, you see, I thought he was talking only, and may be he couldn't do as much as he said, "but for work – there, I can't abide work, and if you'll give me a helping hand in it, I'll thank you."

"Stop," he says, quick as lightning. "I'll help you, and welcome, but if ever you say that to me – if ever you thank me, do you see? – you'll never see me more. Mind that now. I want no thanks, I'll have no thanks, do you hear?" And he stamped his tiddy foot on the earth and looked as wicked as a raging bull.

"Mind that now, great lump as you be," he went on, calming down a bit, "and if ever you need help, or get into trouble, call on me and say, 'Yallery Brown, come from the mools, I want thee!' and I shall be with you to once. And now," says he, and he plucked a dandelion head, "good night to you." And he blowed it up, and it all came in my eyes and ears.

Soon as I could see again, the tiddy creature was gone, and but for the stone on end, and the hole at my feet, I'd have thought I'd been dreaming.

Well, I went home and to bed, and by the morning I'd near forgot all about it. But when I went to the work, there was none to do! All was done already! The horses seen to, the stables cleaned out, everything in its proper place, and I'd nowt to do but sit with my hands in my pockets.

And so it went on day after day, all the work done by Yallery Brown, and better done, too, than I could have done it myself. And if the master gave me more work, I sat down by, and the work did itself, the singeing irons, or the besom, or what not, set to, and with never a hand put to them would get through in no time. For I never saw Yallery Brown in daylight; only in the darklins I have seen him hopping about, like a will-o-the-wyke without his lanthorn.

To first, it was mighty fine for me. I'd nowt to do, and good pay for it; but by and by, things began to go arsy-varsy. If the work was done for me, it was undone for the other lads. If my buckets were filled, theirs were upset. If my tools were sharpened, theirs were blunted and spoiled. If my horses were clean as daisies, theirs were splashed with muck. And so on. Day in, day out, it was always the same. And the lads saw Yallery Brown flitting about of nights, and they saw the things working without hands of days, and they saw as my work was done for me, and theirs undone for them, and naturally they began to look shy on me, and they wouldn't speak or come near me, and they carried tales to the master, and so things went from bad to worse.

For – do you see? – I could do nothing myself. The brooms wouldn't stay in my hand, the plough ran away with me, the hoe kept out of my grip. I'd thought oft as I'd do my own work after all, so as may be Yallery Brown would leave me and my neighbours alone. But I couldn't. I could only sit by and look on, and have the cold shoulder turned on me, whiles the unnatural thing was meddling with the others, and working for me.

To last, things got so bad that the master gave me the sack, and if he hadn't, I do believe all the rest of the lads would have sacked him, for they swore as they'd not stay on the same garth with me. Well, naturally I felt bad. It was a main good place, and good pay, too; and I was fair mad with Yallery Brown, as had got me into such a trouble. So before I knew, I shook my fist in the air and called out as loud as I could:

"Yallery Brown, come from the mools; thou scamp, I want thee!"

You'll scarce believe it, but I'd hardly brung out the words as I felt something tweaking my leg behind, while I jumped with the smart of it. And soon as I looked down, there was the tiddy thing, with its shining hair, and wrinkled face, and wicked, glinting eyes.

I was in a fine rage, and should liked to have kicked him, but it was no good, there wasn't enough of him to get my boot against.

But I said to once: "Look here, master, I'll thank you to leave me alone after this, do you hear? I want none of your help, and I'll have nowt more to do with you – see now."

The horrid thing brak out with a screeching laugh, and pointed his brown finger at me.

"Ho ho, Tom!" says he. "You've thanked me, my lad, and I told you not, I told you not!"

"I don't want your help, I tell you!" I yelled at him. "I only want never to see you again, and to have nowt more to do with you. You can go!"

The thing only laughed and screeched and mocked, as long as I went on swearing, but so soon as my breath gave out, "Tom, my lad," he says with a grin, "I'll tell you summat, Tom. True's true I'll never help you again, and call as you will, you'll never see me after today; but I never said as I'd leave you alone, Tom, and I never will, my lad! I was nice and safe under the stone, Tom, and could do no harm; but you let me out yourself, and you can't put me back again! I would have been your friend and worked for you if you had been wise; but since you are no more than a born fool, I'll give you no more than a born fool's luck; and when all goes arsy-varsy, and everything's a gee – you'll mind as it's Yallery Brown's doing, though happen you didn't see him. Mark my words, will you?"

And he began to sing, dancing round me, like a bairn with his

38

yaller hair, but looking older nor ever with his grinning wrinkled bit of a face:

> "Work as you will,
> "You'll never do well;
> "Work as you might,
> "You'll never gain owt:
> "For harm and mischief and Yallery Brown
> "You've let out yourself from under the stone."

Ay! He said those very words, and they have ringed in my ears ever since, over and over again, like a bell tolling for the burying. And it was the burying of my luck – for I never had any since. However, the imp stood there mocking and grinning at me, and chuckling like the old devil's own wicked self.

And man! – I can't rightly mind what he said next. It was all cussing and swearing; but I was so mazed in fright that I could only stand there, shaking all over me, and staring down at the horrid thing; and I reckon if he'd gone on long, I'd have tumbled down in a fit. But by and by, his yaller shining hair – I can't abide yaller hair since that – rose up in the air, and wrapped itself round him, while he looked for all the world like a great dandelion ball; and he floated away on the wind over the wall and out of sight, with a parting skirl of his wicked voice and sneering laugh.

I tell you, I was near dead with fear, and I can't scarcely tell how I ever got home at all, but I did somehow, I suppose.

Well, that's all; it's not much of a tale, but it's true, every word of it, and there's others besides me as have seen Yallery Brown and known his evil tricks – and did it come true, you say? But it did sure! I have worked here and there, and turned my hand to this and that, but it always went a gee, and it is all Yallery Brown's doing. The children died, and my wife didn't; the beasts never fatted, and nothing ever did well with me. I'm going old now, and I shall must end my days in the house, I reckon; but till I'm dead and buried, and happen even afterwards, there'll be no end to Yallery Brown's spite at me. And day in and day out I hear him saying, whiles I sit here trembling:

> "Work as you will,
> "You'll never do well;
> "Work as you might,
> "You'll never gain owt;
> "For harm and mischief and Yallery Brown
> "You've let out yourself from under the stone."

The
Black
Bull of
Norroway

n Norroway, once, there lived a certain woman, and she had three daughters. The eldest of them said to her mother:

"Mother, bake me a bannock, and roast me a collop, for I'm going away to spotch my fortune."

Her mother did so; and the daughter went away to an old witch washerwife and told her purpose. The old wife bade her stay that day and go and look out of her back door, and see what she could see.

She saw nothing the first day. The second day she did the same, and saw nothing. On the third day she looked again, and saw a coach-and-six coming along the road. She ran in and told the old wife what she saw. "Well," said the old wife, "that's for you." So they took her into the coach, and galloped off.

The second daughter next said to her mother:

"Mother, bake me a bannock, and roast me a collop, for I'm going away to spotch my fortune."

Her mother did so; and away she went to the old witch washer-wife, as her sister had done. So it was as before, and the third day she looked out of the back door, and she saw a coach-and-four coming along the road. "Well," said the old wife, "that's for you." So they took her in, and off they set.

The third daughter said to her mother:

"Mother, bake me a bannock, and roast me a collop, for I'm going away to spotch my fortune."

Her mother did so; and away she went to the old witch washer-wife, who told her to look out of her back door and see what she could see. She did so; and when she came back she said she saw nothing. The second day, she did the same, and saw nothing. The third day, she looked again, and when she came back she said to the old wife that she saw nothing but a great black bull coming crooning along the road. "Well," said the old wife, "that's for you." When she heard this, the girl was next to distracted with grief and terror; but she was lifted up and set on the bull's back, and away they went.

Aye they travelled and on they travelled, till the girl grew faint with hunger.

"Eat out of my right lug," said the black bull, "and drink out of my left lug, and set by your leavings."

She did as he said, and was wonderfully refreshed.

And long they went and sore they went, till they came in sight of a very big and bonny castle.

"Yonder we must be this night," said the bull; "for my old brother lives there."

And presently they were at the place. They lifted her off his back, and took her in, and sent him away to a park for the night.

In the morning, when they brought the bull home, they took the girl into a fine shining parlour, and gave her a beautiful apple, telling her not to break it till her heart was like to break, and over again like to break. Then she was lifted on the bull's back.

And after she had ridden far, and farer than I can tell, they came in sight of a far bonnier castle, and far farther away than the last. The bull said to her:

"Yonder we must be this night, for my second brother lives there."

And they were at the place directly.

They lifted her down, and took her in, and sent the bull to the field.

In the morning, they took her into a fine room and gave her the finest pear she had ever seen, telling her not to break it till her heart was like to break, and over again like to break. Then she was lifted on the bull's back, and away they went.

And long they went and sore they went, till they came in sight of the far biggest castle, and far farest off, they had yet seen.

"Yonder we must be this night," said the bull, "for my young brother lives there."

And straight they were at the place.

They lifted her down, and took her in, and sent the bull to the meadow.

In the morning, they took her into a room, the finest of all, and gave her a plum, telling her not to break it till her heart was like to break, and over again like to break. Then they brought the bull home, set the girl on his back, and away they went.

And long they went and sore they went, till they came to a dark and ugsome glen, where they stopped, and the girl lighted down. The bull said to her:

"Here you must stay till I go and fight with the Old Feller. You must sit yourself on that stone, and move neither hand nor foot till I come back, else I'll never find you again. And if everything round about you turns blue, I have beaten the Old Feller; but should all things turn red, he'll have beaten me."

She sat herself down on the stone, and by and by all around her turned blue. She was overcome with joy, and she lifted the one foot and crossed it over the other, so glad she was that the black bull had won. The bull came and sought her, but never could find her for that.

Long she kept and aye she wept, till she wearied. At last she rose and went away, she knew not where to. On she wandered, till she came to a great hill of glass, that she tried all she could to climb, but was not able. Round the bottom of the hill she went, seeking a passage over, till at last she came to a smith's house; and the smith promised, if she would serve him seven years, he would make her iron shoes, for to climb over the glassy hill.

At seven years' end she got her iron shoes, climbed the glassy hill, and came to the old witch washerwife's house. There she was told of a fine young man that had given some blood-stained shirts to wash, and whoever washed the shirts was to be his wife. The witch had washed; and then she set her daughter to; and both washed, and they washed, and they better washed, in hope of getting the young man; but for all they could do, they could not bring out a single stain.

At length they put the girl to work; and whenever she began, the stains came out pure and clean, and the old witch made the young man believe that it was the daughter had washed the shirts.

So the young man and the daughter were to be married, and the girl was distracted at the thought of it. Then, because her heart was like to break, and over again like to break, she took the apple and broke that. The apple was filled with gold and jewels, the richest she had ever seen; and she showed them to the daughter.

"I will give you all these," she said, "if you will put off the marriage for one day and one night and let me into his room alone."

The daughter took the gold and jewels; but the witch made a sleeping drink, and gave it to the young man. He drank it, and never woke till morning. And all the while, the girl lay by him, sobbing, and singing:

> "Seven long years I served for thee,
> The glassy hill I clomb for thee,
> Thy bloody sark I wrang for thee;
> And wilt thou not waken and turn to me?"

But he did not.

The next day, the girl did not know what to do for grief; she thought that her heart was like to break, and over again like to break; so she broke the pear, and found it filled with gold and jewels far richer than before. She took the gold and jewels to the witch's daughter, and the marriage was put off for one day and one night and she was let into the young man's room all alone; but the old wife gave him another sleeping drink, and he again slept till morning. And through the while the girl lay sighing and singing as before:

> "Seven long years I served for thee,
> The glassy hill I clomb for thee,
> Thy bloody sark I wrang for thee;
> And wilt thou not waken and turn to me?"

Still he slept, and she nearly lost hope altogether.

45

The Black Bull of Norroway

But that morning the young man went out, and he met a shepherd, who asked him what noise and moaning was that he had heard all night from the young man's chamber. The young man said he had heard no noise. But the shepherd said that there was so, and that the young man should stay awake and hear.

The third time the girl thought that her heart was like to break, and over again like to break, so she broke the plum; and inside the plum she found gold and jewels by far the farthest rich of all, and she gave them to the daughter to put off the marriage for another day and another night, and for herself to be with the young man in his room alone. The witch gave the young man another sleeping drink, but he told her he could not drink it that night without sweetening; and when she went away to fetch honey for the drink, he poured it out, and made her think that he had drunk it, after all. Then he went to his bed.

The girl came and lay by him, and sang:

> "Seven long years I served for thee,
> The glassy hill I clomb for thee,
> Thy bloody sark I wrang for thee;
> O, my bonny bull of Norroway,
> Wilt thou not waken and turn to me?"

He heard, and turned to her. And she told him all that had happened to her, and he told her all that had happened to him. And he had the old witch washerwife and her daughter burnt, and he himself and the girl were married, and they are living happy till this day, for all I know.

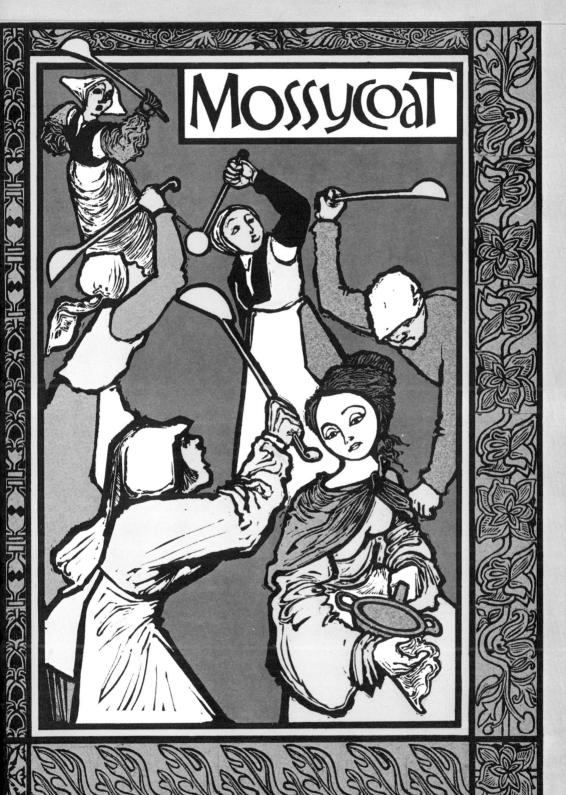

here was once a poor old widow-woman as lived in a little cottage. She had a daughter, and she was very beautiful. Her mother was busy every day, a-spinning of a coat for her.

A hawker came courting this girl; came regular, he did, and kept on a-bringing of her this thing and that. He was in love with her, and badly wanted her to marry him. But she wasn't in love with him; it didn't fall out like that, and she was in a puzzlement what she'd best do about him. So one day she asked her mother.

"Let him come," her mother told her, "and get what you can out of him, while I finish this coat, after when you won't have no need of him, nor his presents, neither. So tell him, girl, as you won't marry him, unless he gets you a dress of white satin with sprigs of gold on it as big as a man's hand; and mind as you tell him it must fit exactly."

Next time the hawker came round, and asked her to wed him, the girl told him just this, the very same as her mother had said. He took stock of her size and build, the hawker did; and inside of a week he was back with the dress. It answered the describance all right, and when the girl went upstairs with her mother, and tried it on, it fitted her exactly.

"What should I do now, Mother?" she asked.

"Tell him," her mother said, "as you won't marry him unless he gets you a dress made of silk the colour of all the birds of the air; and as before, it must fit you exactly."

The girl told the hawker this, and in two or three days he was back at the cottage, with this coloured silk dress the girl had asked for; and being as he knew the size from the other one, of course it fitted her exactly.

"Now what should I do, Mother?" she asked.

"Tell him," her mother said, "as you won't marry him unless he gets you a pair of silver slippers as fits you exactly.''

The girl told the hawker so, and in a few days he called round with them. The slippers fitted her exactly; they were not too tight, neither were they too big or loose. Again the girl asked her mother what she should do now.

"I can finish the coat tonight,'' her mother said, "so you can tell the hawker you'll marry him tomorrow, and he's to be here at ten o'clock.''

So the girl told him this. "Think-on, my dear,'' she says, "ten o'clock in the morning.''

"I'll be there, my love,'' he says. "I shall.''

That night her mother was at work on the coat till late, but she finished it all right. Green moss and gold thread, that's what it was made of; just them two things. "Mossycoat'' she called it, and gave the name to her daughter. It was a magic coat, she said, a wishing coat, she told her daughter. When she'd got it on, she told her she'd only to wish to be somewhere, and she'd be there that very instant.

Next morning the mother was up by the time it was light. She called her daughter, and told her she must now go into the world and seek her fortune, and a handsome fortune it was to be. She was a foreseer, the old mother was, and knew what was a-coming. She gave her daughter mossycoat to put under her other clothes, and a gold crown for her head to take with her, and she told her to take as well the two dresses and the silver slippers she'd had off the hawker. But she was to go in the clothes she wore every day, her working clothes, that is.

And now she's ready for to start, Mossycoat is. Her mother then tells her she is to wish herself a hundred miles away, and then walk on till she comes to a big hall, and there she's to ask for a job. "You won't have far to walk, my blessed,'' the mother says. "And they'll be sure to find you work at this big hall.''

Mossycoat did as her mother told her, and soon she found herself in front of a fine gentleman's house. She knocked at the front door and said she was looking for work. Well, the long and the short of it was the mistress herself came to see her; and she liked the look of her, the lady did.

"What work can you do?" she asked.

"I can cook, your ladyship," said Mossycoat. "In fact, I'm in the way of being a very good cook, from what people have remarked."

"I can't give you a job as cook," the lady tells her, "being as I've got one already; but I'd be willing to employ you to help the cook, if so as you'd be satisfied with that."

"Thank you, ma'am," says Mossycoat. "I'd be real glad of the place."

So it was settled she was to be undercook. And after when the lady had shown her up to her bedroom, she took her to the kitchen, and introduced her to the other servants.

"This is Mossycoat," she tells them, "and I've engaged her," she says, "to be undercook."

She leaves them then, the mistress does; and Mossycoat she goes up to her bedroom again, to unpack her things, and hide away her gold crown and silver slippers, and her silk and satin dresses.

The other kitchen girls were fair beside theirselves with jealousy; and it didn't mend matters that the new girl was a sight beautifuller than what any of them were. Here was this vagrant in rags put above them, when all she was fit for at best was to be scullery girl. If anybody was to be undercook, it stands to sense it should be one of them as really knew about things, not this girl in rags and tatters, picked up off the roads. But they'd put her in her place, they would. So they go on and on, till Mossycoat comes down ready to start work. Then they set on her. Who did she think she was? She'd be undercook, would she? No fear! What she'd have to do, and all she was fit for, was to scour the pans, clean the knives, do the grates and suchlike; and all she'd get was this. And down came the skimmer on top of her head, pop, pop, pop.

"That's what you deserve," they tell her, "and that's what you can expect, my lady."

And that's how it was with Mossycoat. She was put to do all the dirtiest work, and soon she was up to her ears in grease, and her face as black as soot. And every now and again, first one and then another of the servants would pop, pop, pop her on the head with the skimmer, till the poor girl's head was that sore, she couldn't hardly abide it.

Well, it got on, and it got on, and still Mossycoat was at her pans, and knives, and grates; and still the servants were pop, pop, popping her on the head with the skimmer.

Now there was a big dance coming, as was to last three nights, with hunting and other sports in the daytime. All the headmost people for miles round were to be there; and the master and mistress, and the young master, of course they were going. It was all the talk of the servants, this dance was. One was wishing she could be there; another would like to dance with some of the young lords; a third would like to see the ladies' dresses; and so they went on, all excepting Mossycoat. If only they had the clothes, they'd be all right, they thought, as they considered theirselves as good as high-titled ladies any day.

"And you, Mossycoat, you'd like to go, wouldn't you now?" they say. "A fit person you'd be there in all your rags and dirt," they say, and down comes the skimmer on her head, pop, pop, pop. Then they laugh at her; which goes to show what a low class of people they were.

Now Mossycoat, as I've said before, was very handsome, and rags and dirt couldn't hide that. The other servants might think that they did, but the young master had had his eye on her, and the master and mistress, they had always taken particular notice of her, on account of her good looks. When the big dance was coming on, they thought it would be nice to ask her to go to it; so they sent for her to see if she'd like to.

"No, thank you," she says, "I'd never think of such a thing. I know my place better than that," she says. "Besides, I'd greasy all the one side of the coach," she tells them, "and anybody's clothes I came up against."

They make light of that, and press her to go, the master and mistress do. It's very kind of them, Mossycoat says, but she's not for going, she says, and she sticks to that.

When she gets back into the kitchen, you may depend on it, the other servants want to know why she'd been sent for. Had she got notice, or what was it? So she told them the master and mistress had asked her would she like to go to the dance with them. "What? You?" they say. "It's unbelievable. If it had been one of us now, that would be different. But you! Why, you'd never be allowed in; you'd greasy all the gentlemen's clothes, if there were any who would dance with a scullery girl; and the ladies, they'd be forced to hold their noses when they passed by you, to be sure they would." No, they couldn't believe, they said, that the master and mistress had ever asked her to go to the ball with them. She must be lying, they said, and down came the skimmer a-top of her head, pop, pop, pop.

Next night, the master and the mistress and their son, this time, asked her to go to the dance. It was a grand affair the night before, they said, and she should have been there. It was going to be still grander tonight, they said, and they begged her to come with them, especially the young master. But no, she says, on account of her rags and her grease and dirt, she couldn't, and she wouldn't; and even the young master couldn't persuade her, though it wasn't for the want of trying. The other servants just didn't believe her when she told them about her being invited again to the dance, and about the young master being very pressing.

"Hark to her!" they say. "What will the upstart say next? And all lies," they say. Then one of them, with a mouth like a pig-trough, and legs like a cart horse, catches hold of the skimmer, and down it comes, pop, pop, pop, on Mossycoat's head.

That night, Mossycoat decided she would go to the dance, in right proper style, all on her own, and without nobody knowing it. The first thing she does is to put all the other servants into a trance; she just touches each of them, unnoticed, as she moves about, and they all fall asleep under a spell as soon as she does, and can't wake up again on their own; the spell has to be broken by somebody with the power, same as she has through her magic coat, or has got it some other way.

Next Mossycoat has a real good wash: she'd never been allowed to before since she'd been at the hall, since the other servants were determined to make and to keep her as greasy and dirty as they could. Then she goes upstairs to her bedroom, throws off her working clothes and shoes, and puts on her white satin dress with the gold sprigs, her silver slippers, and her gold crown. Of course, she had mossycoat on underneath. So as soon as she was ready, she just wished herself at the dance, and there she was, very near as soon as the wish was spoken. She did just feel herself rising up and flying through the elements, but only for a moment. Then she was in the ballroom.

The young master sees her standing there, and once he catches sight of her he can't take his eyes off her; he'd never seen anybody as handsome before, or as beautifully dressed. "Who is she?" he asks his mother; but she doesn't know, she tells him.

"Can't you find out, Mother?" he says. "Can't you go and talk to her?"

His mother sees he'll never rest till she does, so she goes and introduces herself to the young lady, and asks her who she is, where she comes from, and such as that; but all she could get out of her was that she came from a place where they hit her on the head with a skimmer.

Then presently, the young master he goes over and introduces himself, but she doesn't tell him her name nor nothing; and when he asks her to have a dance with him, she says no, she'd rather not. He stops beside her, though, and keeps asking her time and again, and at the finish she says she will, and links up with him. They dance once, up and down the room; then she says she must go. He presses her to stop, but it's a waste of breath; she's determined to go, there and then.

"All right," he says – there was nothing else he could say – "I'll come and see you off." But she just wished she was at home, and there she was. No seeing her off for the young master, there wasn't, she just went from his side in the twinkle of an eye, leaving him standing there gaping with wonderment. Thinking she might be in the hall, or the porch, a-waiting of her carriage, he goes to see, but there's no sign of her anywhere inside or out, and nobody he asked had seen her go. He went back to the ballroom, but he can't think of nothing or nobody but her, and all the time he's a-wanting to go home.

When Mossycoat is back home, she makes sure that all the other servants are still in a trance. Then she goes and changes into her working get-up; and after when she'd done that, she came down into the kitchen again, and touched each of the servants.

That wakens them, as you might say; anyway, they start up, wondering whatever time of day it is, and how long they've been asleep. Mossycoat tells them, and drops a hint she may have to let the mistress know. They beg of her not to let on about them, and most of them think to give her presents if she won't tell. Old things they were, but with a bit of wear in them still – a skirt, a pair of shoes, stockings, stays, and what not. So Mossycoat promises that she won't tell on them. And that night they don't hit her on the head with the skimmer.

All next day the young master is unrestful. He can't settle his mind to nothing but the young lady he fell in love with at the very first sight of her. He was wondering all the time would she be there again tonight, and would she vanish the same as she did last night; and thinking how he could stop her, or catch up with her if she was for doing this a second time. He must find out where she lives, he thinks, else how is he to go on after when the dance is over? He'd die, he tells his mother, if he can't get her for his wife; he's that madly in love with her.

"Well," says his mother, "I thought she was a nice modest girl, but she wouldn't say who or what she was, or where she came from, except it was a place where they hit her on the head with a skimmer."

"She's a bit of a mystery, I know," says the young master, "but that doesn't signify I want her any the less. I must have her, Mother," he says, "whoever and whatever she is; and that's the dear truth, Mother, strike me dead if it isn't."

Women servants have long ears, and big mouths, and you may be sure it wasn't long before the young master and this wonderful handsome lady he'd fallen in love with were all the talk in the kitchen.

"And fancy you, Mossycoat, thinking he specially wanted you to go to the dance," they say, and start in on her proper, making all manner of nasty sarcastical remarks, and hitting her on the head with the skimmer, pop, pop, pop, for lying to them (as they said). It was the same again later on, when the master and mistress had sent for her, and asked her once more to go to the dance with them, and once more she'd refused. It was her last chance, they said – that was the servants – and a lot more besides that isn't worth repeating. And down came the skimmer a-top of her head, pop, pop, pop. Then she put the whole breed of them into a trance like she had done the night before, and she got herself ready to go the dance; the only difference being that this time she put her other dress on, the one made of silk the colour of all the birds of the air.

She's in the ballroom now, Mossycoat is. The young master, he's waiting and watching for her. As soon as he sees her, he asks his father to send for the fastest horse in the stable, and have it kept standing ready saddled at the door. Then he asks his mother to go over and talk to the young lady for a bit. She does that, but can't learn no more about her than she did the night before.

Then the young master hears that his horse is ready at the door; so he goes over to the young lady and asks her for a dance. She says just the same as the night before, "No," at first, but "Yes," at the finish, and just as then, she says she must go after when they've danced only once the length of the room and back. But this time he keeps hold of her till they get outside. Then she wishes herself at home, and is there nearly as soon as she has spoken.

The young master felt her rise into the air, but couldn't do nothing to stop her. But perhaps he did just touch her foot, because she dropped one slipper; I couldn't be sure that he did; it looks a bit like it, though. He picks the slipper up; but as for catching her, it would be easier by far to catch the wind on a blowy night.

As soon as she gets home, Mossycoat changes back into her old things; then she looses the other servants from the spell she'd put on them. They've been asleep again, they think, and offer Mossycoat one a shilling, another half a crown, another a week's wages, if she won't tell on them; and she promises she won't.

The young master is in bed next day, a-dying for the love of the lady that lost one of her silver slippers the night before. The doctors can't do him not the least good. So it was given out what his state was, and that it was only the lady able to wear the slipper as could save his life; and if she would come forward, he would marry her.

Ladies came from near and far, some with big feet and some with small, but none small enough to get it on however much they pinched and squeezed. Poorer people came as well, but it was just the same with them. And of course, all the servants tried, but they were out of it altogether. The young master was a-dying. Was there nobody else, his mother asked, nobody at all, rich or poor? "No," they told her; everybody had tried it excepting it was Mossycoat.

"Tell her to come at once," says the mistress.

So they fetched her.

"Try this slipper on," she says – that's the mistress.

Mossycoat gets her foot into it easy enough; it fits her exactly. The young master jumps out of bed, and is just a-going to take her in his arms.

"Stop," says Mossycoat, and runs off; but before long she's back again in her satin dress with gold sprigs, her gold crown, and both her silver slippers. The young master is just a-going to take her in his arms. "Stop," she says, and again she runs off. This time she comes back in her silk dress the colour of all the birds of the air. She doesn't stop him this time, and he nearly eats her.

After when they have all settled down again, and are talking quiet-like, there are one or two things the master and mistress and the young master would like to know. How did she get to dance, and back again, in no time, they asked her. "Just wishing," she says; and she tells them all about the magic coat her mother had made for her, and the powers it gave her if she cared to use them.

"Yes, that explains everything," they say.

Then they bethink themselves of her saying as she came from where they hit her on the head with a skimmer. What did she mean by that, they want to know. She meant just what she said, she told them; it was always coming down on her head, pop, pop, pop.

They were right angry when they heard that, and the whole of the kitchen servants were told to go, and the dogs were sent after them to drive the varmints right away from the place.

As soon as they could, Mossycoat and the young master got married, and she had a coach and six to ride in – no, ten if she liked; for you may be sure she had everything she fancied. They lived happy ever after, and had a basketful of children. I was there, playing the fiddle, when their oldest son came of age. But that was many years back, and I shouldn't wonder if the old master and mistress aren't dead by now, though I've never heard tell as they were.

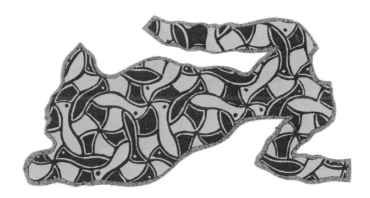

Kate Crackernuts

nce upon a time there was a king and a queen, as in many lands have been. The king had a daughter, and the queen had a daughter. The queen was jealous of the king's daughter, for being bonnier than her own, and she cast about to spoil her beauty.

So the queen took counsel of the henwife. "Send the lassie to me in the morning to get eggs," said the henwife, "and send her fasting."

The queen did so; but the lassie found a crust of bread to eat before she went out. When she came to the henwife's, she asked for eggs.

"Lift the lid off that pot there, and see," said the henwife.

She lifted the lid off the pot, but nothing happened.

"Go home to your minnie," said the henwife, "and tell her to keep the press door better steekit."

The lassie went back home and told the queen what the henwife had said; so the queen watched her the next morning, and sent her away fasting. But the lassie picked a handful of wheat at the road side, and ate it by the way. Then she went to the henwife, and asked for the eggs.

"Lift the lid off that pot there, and see," said the henwife.

The lassie lifted the lid off the pot, but nothing happened.

"Go home to your minnie," said the henwife, "and tell her the pot won't boil if the fire's away."

So the lassie went home and told the queen.

The next day the queen herself took the lassie to the henwife; and when the lid was lifted, off jumped the lassie's own bonnie head, and on jumped a sheep's. The queen was pleased.

But the queen's daughter, Kate, took a fine linen cloth and wrapped it round her sister's head, and took her by the hand, and went out to seek their fortune.

They went, and they went far, till they came to a king's house. Kate knocked at the door and called, "A night's lodging for me and a sick sister!"

"You'll get that," said the king, "if you'll sit up with my sick son."

"I will," said Kate.

"There'll be a peck of silver for you," said the king, "if all's right."

So Kate sat up by the sick prince's bed; and all went well till midnight. Then, as twelve o'clock was ringing, the prince rose and dressed himself and went downstairs. Kate followed.

The prince went to the stable, saddled his horse, called his hound, jumped into the saddle, and Kate leapt lightly up behind.

Away rode the prince and Kate through the greenwood, Kate, as they pass, plucking nuts from the trees and filling her apron.

They rode on and on till they came to a green hill. The prince here drew bridle and said, "Open, open, green hill, and let the young prince in with his horse and his hound." And added Kate, "His lady him behind."

The green hill opened and they passed in.

Inside the hill there was a hall, brightly lighted up, and many beautiful ladies took the prince and led him off to the dance; while Kate, unperceived, sat herself by the door. There she saw the prince dancing, dancing, dancing till he could dance no longer and fell upon the floor, when the ladies would fan him and kiss him, and he rose again to go on dancing.

Then the cock crew, and the prince made all haste to get on horseback, Kate leaping lightly up behind, and home they rode, and Kate sat down by the fire, and cracked her nuts, and ate them.

The king said, "How is the sick prince?"

"He will be better yet," said Kate.

"Sit up with him again," said the king. "There'll be a peck of gold, if all's right."

So Kate sat with the sick prince a second night, and all happened as it had the first. Away rode the prince and Kate through the greenwood, Kate, as they pass, plucking nuts from the trees and filling her apron. They came to the green hill, and the prince said, "Open, open, green hill, and let the young prince in with his horse and his hound." And added Kate, "His lady him behind."

The green hill opened, and the beautiful ladies led the prince off to the dance, while Kate, unperceived, sat herself by the door.

She saw a bairnie playing with a wand, and one of the ladies said, "Three strakes of that wand would make Kate's sick sister as bonnie as ever she was."

So Kate rolled nuts to the bairnie, and rolled nuts till the bairnie toddled after the nuts and let fall the wand, and Kate took it up and put it in her apron.

Then the cock crew, and the prince made all haste to get on horseback, Kate leaping lightly up behind, and home they rode, and Kate sat down by the fire, and cracked her nuts, and ate them.

The king said, "How is the sick prince?"

"He will be better yet," said Kate.

"Sit up with him again," said the king.

"If I can have him to wed."

"You'll get that, if all's right."

So Kate sat with the sick prince a third night, and away they rode, the prince and Kate, through the greenwood, Kate, as they pass, plucking nuts from the trees and filling her apron. The green hill opened and they passed in, and the prince danced, and Kate, unperceived, sat herself by the door.

The bairnie was playing with a birdie, and one of the ladies said, "Three bites of that birdie would make the sick prince as well as ever he was."

So Kate rolled nuts to the bairnie, and rolled nuts till the bairnie toddled after the nuts and let fall the birdie, and Kate took it up and put it in her apron.

Then the cock crew, and the prince made all haste to get on horseback, Kate leaping lightly up behind, and home they rode; and

Kate plucked the feathers off, and cooked the birdie.

"Oh the smell!" said the sick prince, "I wish I had a bite of that birdie."

So Kate gave him a bite of the birdie, and he rose up on his elbow.

By and by he cried out again, "Oh, if I had another bite of that birdie."

So Kate gave him another bite, and he sat up on his bed.

Then he said again. "Oh, if I had a third bite of that birdie."

So Kate gave him a third bite, and he forgot the green hill. He dressed himself, and sat down by the fire, and when the king came he found Kate and the young prince cracking nuts together.

Kate took, the wand and gave her sister three strakes of it, and the sheep's head fell off, and her own head was on again, and the king's second son saw her and fell in love with her.

So the sick son married the well sister, and the well son married the sick sister.

> They lived long,
> And died happy,
> And never drank out
> Of a dry cappy.

The BaTTle of the BIRDS

here was once a time when every creature and bird was gathering to battle. The son of the king of Tethertown said that he would go to see the battle and that he would bring sure word home who would be the champion among them this year.

The battle was over before he arrived, all but one fight between a black raven and a snake; and it seemed as if the snake would get the victory over the raven. When the king's son saw this, he helped the raven and with one blow swept the head off the snake; and the raven said, "For your kindness to me this day, I will give you a sight. Come up now on the root of my two wings." The king's son mounted upon the raven, and before it stopped it took him over seven bens, and seven glens, and seven mountain moors.

"Now," said the raven, "do you see that house yonder? Go to it. It is a sister of mine that lives there, and I will go bail that you are welcome. If she asks you were you at the battle of the birds, say that you were. And if she asks you did you see my likeness, say that you did. But be sure you meet me tomorrow morning here, in this place."

The king's son got good and right good treatment that night: meat of each meat, drink of each drink, warm water to his feet, and a soft bed for his limbs.

On the next day the raven gave him the same sight over seven bens, and seven glens, and seven mountain moors. They saw a house far off, but, though far, they were soon there. The king's son got good treatment this night, as before; meat and drink, warm water to his feet, and a soft bed to his limbs; and on the day after that it was the same thing.

But the third morning, instead of the raven, he met the handsomest lad he ever saw, with a bundle in his hand. The king's son asked the lad if he had seen a big black raven. And the lad said to him, "You will never see the raven again; for I am that raven. I was put under spells; it was meeting you that loosed me, and for that you are getting this bundle. Now," said the lad, "you will turn back on the self-same steps, and you will lie a night in each house, as you were before; but your lot is not to open the bundle till you are in the place where you would most wish to dwell."

The king's son turned his back to the lad, and his face to his father's house; and he got lodging from the raven's sisters, just as he got it when going forward.

Now when he was nearing his father's house he was going through a close wood, and it seemed to him that the bundle was growing heavy, and he thought he would look what was in it. He opened the bundle, but not without astonishing himself. On an instant he saw the very grandest place he ever saw: a great castle, and an orchard about the castle, in which was every kind of fruit and herb.

He stood full of wonder and regret for having opened the bundle – it was not in his power to put it back again – and he would have wished this place to be in the little green hollow that was opposite his father's house. But at one glance, he saw a giant coming.

"It is a bad place where you have built your house, king's son," said the giant.

"Yes, but it is not here I would wish it to be," said the king's son.

"What is the reward for putting it back in the bundle as before?" said the giant.

"What is the reward you would ask?" said the king's son.

"I would ask for you to give me the first son you have, when he is seven years of age," said the giant.

"You will get that, if I have him," said the king's son.

In a twinkling the giant put each garden, and orchard, and castle in the bundle as they were before.

"Now," said the giant, "take you your own road, and I will take my road; but mind your promise, and though you should forget, I will remember."

The Battle of the Birds

The king's son took the road, and at the end of a few days he reached the place he was fondest of. He opened the bundle, and all was just as it had been. And when he opened the door of the castle he saw the most beautiful woman in the world.

"Advance, king's son," said the woman; "everything is in order for you, if you will marry me this very night."

"I am the man that is willing," said the king's son. And on that same night they were married, and soon the king died and his son was crowned king after him.

Now the new king and his queen were happy, and before long they had between them a son. But at the end of seven years and a day the giant came to the castle. The king remembered his promise, and till now he had not told that promise to the queen.

When the queen heard of it, she said, "Leave the matter between me and the giant."

"Turn out your son," said the giant; "mind your promise."

"You shall get that," said the king, "when his mother puts him in order for his journey."

The queen arrayed the cook's son, and she gave him to the giant by the hand. The giant took him, but he had not gone far when he gave the boy a rod, and said, "If your father had that rod, what would he do with it?"

The boy said, "If my father had this rod, he would beat the dogs and the cats for going near the king's meat."

"You are the cook's son," said the giant; and he caught him by the two ankles and knocked him – Sgleog! – against the stone of the road. Then he turned back to the castle in rage and madness, and he said that if they did not send out the king's son to him, the highest stone of the castle would be the lowest.

"We'll try it yet," said the queen; and she arrayed the butler's son, and gave him to the giant.

The giant had not gone far when he put the rod in the boy's hand. "If your father had that rod," said the giant, "what would he do with it?"

The boy said, "If my father had this rod, he would beat the dogs and the cats for coming near the king's bottles and glasses."

"You are the son of the butler," said the giant, and he knocked his brains out, too. Then he turned back to the castle in rage and madness; the earth shook under the sole of his foot, and the castle shook, and all that was in it.

"Out here your son!" said the giant. "Or in a twinkling the stone that is highest shall be the lowest!"

So they had to give the king's son to the giant.

The giant took him to his own house, and he reared him as his own son. On a day of days, when the giant was from home, the lad heard the sweetest music he ever heard in a room at the top of the house, and at a glance he saw the finest face of a girl he had ever seen. The girl beckoned to him to come nearer, and she told him to go this time, but to be sure to be at the same place about that dead midnight.

And as he promised, he did. The giant's daughter was out and at his side, and she said, "Tomorrow you will get the choice of my two sisters to marry; then say you that you will not take either, but me. My father wants me to marry the son of the king of the Green Town, but I don't like him."

On the morrow, the giant took out his three daughters, and he said, "Now, son of the king of Tethertown, you have not lost by living with me so long. You will get to wife one of my two eldest daughters and, with her, leave to go home with her the day after the wedding."

"If you will give me the pretty little one here," said the king's son, "I shall take you at your word."

The giant's wrath kindled, and he said, "Before you get her, you must do the three things that I ask you to do."

"Say on," said the king's son.

The giant took him to the byre. "Now," said the giant, "the dung of the hundred cattle is here, and it has not been cleansed for seven years. I am going from home today, and if this byre is not cleansed before night comes, so clean that this golden apple will run from end to end of it, not only shall you not get my daughter, but a drink of your blood will quench my thirst this night.''

The king's son began to cleanse the byre, but it was just as well to keep baling the great ocean. After mid-day, when sweat was blinding him, the giant's young daughter came where he was, and she said to him, "You are being punished, king's son."

"I am that," said the king's son.

"Come over," said she, "and lay down your weariness."

"I will do that," said he. "There is but death awaiting me, at any rate."

He sat down near her. He was so tired that he fell asleep beside her. She took the golden apple, and said, "Gather, o shovel! And put out, o grape!" And when he awoke, the byre was so well cleansed that the golden apple would run from end to end of it. "Keep you the golden apple," said the giant's daughter.

In came the giant, and he said, "Have you cleansed the byre, king's son?"

"I have," said he.

"Somebody has," said the giant.

"It was not you, at all events," said the king's son.

"Yes, yes!" said the giant. "Since you were so active today, you will get from now to this time tomorrow to thatch the byre with the down of birds – birds with no two feathers of one colour."

The king's son was on foot before the day; he caught up his bow and his quiver of arrows to kill the birds. He took to the moors; but if he did, the birds were not easy to hit. He ran after them until the sweat was blinding him.

About mid-day, the giant's young daughter came. "You are spending yourself," she said.

"I am," said he. "There have fallen only these two blackbirds, and both of one colour."

"Come over and lay down your weariness on this pretty hillock," said the giant's daughter.

"Willingly," said he. "There is but death at the end." And he was not long there till he fell asleep.

When he awoke, the giant's daughter had gone. He thought he would go back to the house, and there he saw the byre, thatched with feathers, no two of one colour.

The giant came in. "Have you thatched the byre, king's son?" he said.

"I thatched it," said he.

"Somebody thatched it," said the giant.

"You did not thatch it," said the king's son.

"Yes, yes!" said the giant.

"Now," said the giant, "there is a fir tree beside the lake down there, and in its top a magpie's nest. You will find eggs in the nest; and I must have them for my first meal. Not one must be burst or broken, and there are five in the nest."

Early in the morning, the king's son went where the tree was, and that tree was not hard to hit upon. Its match was not in the whole wood. From the foot to the first branch was five hundred feet.

The king's son went round and round about the tree. The giant's daughter came, and she said, "You are losing the skin of your hands and feet."

"I am," said he. "I am no sooner up than down."

"This is no time for stopping," said the giant's daughter.

She thrust finger after finger of her fingers into the tree, until she made a ladder for the king's son to go up to the magpie's nest. When he was at the nest, she said, "Make haste now with the eggs, for my father's breath is burning my back." In the hurry, she left her little finger in the top of the tree.

"Now," said she, "you will go home with the eggs quickly, and you will get me to marry tonight if you can know me. I and my sisters will be in the like garments; but look at me when my father says, 'Go to your wife, king's son.' And you will see a hand without a little finger."

The giant came and said, "Have you the eggs, king's son?"

"I have," said he.

"Somebody had them," said the giant.

"It was not you," said the king's son.

"Yes, yes!" said the giant. "Be making ready for your marriage."

Then indeed there was a wedding, and it was a wedding! Giants and gentlemen, and the son of the king of the Green Town were in the midst. The dancing began, and that was the dancing! The giant's house shook from top to bottom. But bed time came, and the giant said, "It is time for you to go to rest, son of the king of Tethertown; take your bride with you from among those."

The giant's daughter put out the hand from which the little finger was missing, and the king's son took hold.

"You have aimed well, this time too," said the giant; "yet there is no knowing but we may meet you another way."

They went to rest.

"Now," said she, "sleep not, or else you die. We must fly quick, quick, or for certain my father will kill you."

They went out and mounted the blue grey filly in the stable. "Stop awhile," said the giant's daughter, "and I shall play a trick on the old hero."

She went and put a wooden bench in the bed of the king's son, and two wooden benches in her own. She spat at the front of her own bed, and spat at the side of the giant's bed, and spat at the passage door; and she set two green apples above the giant's bed, ready to fall on him when he should wake. Then she mounted the filly behind her husband, and they set the filly running with might.

The giant awoke, and shouted, "Rise, daughter, and bring me a drink of blood from the king's son."

"I will arise," said the spittle by his daughter's bed; and one of the apples fell and struck him between the two shoulders, and he slept.

The second time it was, "Rise, wife!"

"I will arise," said the spittle by the giant's bed; and the second apple fell and set him sleeping.

Then a third time, "Are you rising to fetch me the drink?" said the giant.

70

"I have arisen," said the spittle by the passage door.

Then the giant lay a while, and got up with an axe, and struck it into the bench on the bed of the king's son. And when he saw what he had, he ran to his daughter's bed and struck his axe into the two benches there. Then he ran into the stable and said, "My own daughter's tricks are trying me. Here's after them!" he said.

At the mouth of day, the giant's daughter said, "My father's breath is burning my back. Put your hand in the ear of the grey filly, and whatever you find there, throw it behind us."

"There is a twig of sloe tree," said the king's son.

"Throw it behind us," said she.

No sooner did he than there were twenty miles of black thorn wood, so thick that a weasel could not go through it. The giant came headlong, and fleeced his face and neck in the thorns.

The giant said, "If I had my big axe and my little axe, I should not be long making a way through this."

He went home for the big axe and the little axe, and he was not long in making a way through the black thorn.

"I shall leave the big axe and the little axe here till I return," he said.

"If you leave them," said a hoodie in a tree, "we shall steal them."

"You may do that," said the giant, "but I will set them home." He went back and left them at the house.

At the heat of the day, the giant's daughter said, "My father's breath is burning my back. Put your finger in the filly's ear and throw behind you what you find there."

The king's son got a splinter of grey stone. He threw it behind him, and there were twenty miles, by breadth and height, of great grey rock between them and the giant. The giant came full pelt, but past the rock he could not go.

"The tricks of my daughter are the hardest things that ever met me," said the giant; "but if I had my big mattock and my little mattock, I should not be long about this rock also."

He went home for the big mattock and the little mattock, and he was not long in making a road through the rock.

"I shall leave the big mattock and the little mattock here, and I shall return no more," said the giant.

"If you leave them," said a hoodie, "we shall steal them."

"Do that," said the giant. "There is no time to go back."

At dusk, the giant's daughter said, "My father's breath is burning my back. Look in the filly's ear, king's son, or else we are lost."

He did so, and it was a bladder of water he found this time. He threw it behind him, and there was a lake, twenty miles in length and breadth between them and the giant.

The giant said, "If I had my big scoop and my little scoop, this lake would soon be dry."

He went home for the big scoop and the little scoop, and he was not long in making the lake dry.

"I shall leave the big scoop and the little scoop here, and I shall return no more," said the giant.

"If you leave them," said a hoodie, "we shall steal them."

"There is no time to go back," said the giant.

The giant ran on. Seven miles at a stride, he took, and he saw seven miles around him by the light of his sword.

"Have you the golden apple?" said the giant's daughter.

"I have," said the king's son.

"Then throw it beneath the filly's hooves," said the giant's daughter. "There is no other."

The king's son dropped the golden apple, and it was crushed beneath the filly's hooves; and straightaway the giant fell dead, for his life was there.

The giant's daughter and the king's son rode through the night, and in the morning they came to the outskirts of Tethertown.

"You go on," said the giant's daughter, "but do not suffer any man or creature to kiss you; for, if you do, you will not remember that you have ever seen me."

So the king's son went to his father's castle, and he charged his father and his mother not to kiss him; but as mishap was to be, an old greyhound knew him, and had not forgotten him, and it jumped up to his mouth; and after that he did not remember the giant's daughter.

She was sitting at the well's side as he left her, but the king's son did not come back. At nightfall she climbed up into a tree of oak that grew over the well, and she lay in the fork of the tree until day.

A shoemaker had a house near the well, and in the morning he asked his wife to go for a drink for him out of the well. When the shoemaker's wife reached the well, and when she saw the shadow of the giant's daughter in the tree, thinking of it that it was her own shadow – though she never thought till now that she was so handsome – she dropped the dish that was in her hand so that it was broken on the ground, and she took herself back to the house without dish or water.

"Where is the water, wife?" said the shoemaker.

"You shambling, contemptible carle without grace," said his wife, "I have stayed too long your water and wood thrall!"

"Go," said the shoemaker to his daughter, "and fetch me a drink from the well."

His daughter went, and in the same way so it happened to her. She never thought till now that she was so beautiful, and she took herself home.

"Where is the drink?" said the shoemaker.

"You coarse-cloth shoe carle, do you think that I am no better than to be your thrall?"

The shoemaker thought that his women had taken a turn in their understanding, and he went himself to the well. He saw the shadow of the girl in the well, and he looked up to the tree, and he saw the finest woman he ever saw.

"Your seat is wavering," said the shoemaker, "but your face is fair. Come down, for there is need of you for a while at my house."

The shoemaker took her to his house, and he gave her to share all that was in it. And in a day or two, there came a leash of gentlemen lads to have shoes made for them, for the king's son had come home, and he was going to marry.

"You have a pretty daughter here," said the lads.

"She is pretty," said the shoemaker, "but she is no daughter of mine."

"I would give a hundred pounds to marry her," said one of the lads. And two others said the same.

The shoemaker said that he had nothing to do with her.

"But," said they, "ask her tonight, and send us word tomorrow."

When the gentlemen lads went away, the giant's daughter asked the shoemaker what they were saying about her. The shoemaker told her.

"You go after them," she said. "I shall marry one of them, and let him bring his purse with him."

The shoemaker went after them, and he told them that. One lad returned, and he gave the shoemaker a hundred pounds.

The giant's daughter and the lad went to rest, and when she had laid down she asked the lad for a drink of water from a tumbler that was on the further side of the room. He went; but his hands stuck fast to the tumbler and out of that he could not come, and he held the tumbler of water all night, and in the morning she asked the shoemaker to take away the lubberly boy.

So that wooer went, but he did not tell the other two how it had happened to him. And next came the second lad, and in the same way, when she had gone to rest, "Look," said the giant's daughter, "and make sure the latch is on." The latch laid hold of his hands, and out of that he could not come the length of the night, and out of that he did not come till the morrow's day. He went under shame and disgrace.

No matter, he did not tell the third lad how it had happened, and on the third night he came. As it happened to the two others, so it happened to him. One foot stuck to the floor; he could neither come nor go; and in the morning he was set free, and he was not seen once looking behind him.

"Now," said the giant's daughter to the shoemaker, "here are the purses of gold; I have no need of them. It will better you, and I shall be no worse for your kindness to me."

And on that very day the king's son was to be married.

"I should like to get a sight of the king's son before he marries," said the giant's daughter.

"Come with me," said the shoemaker, "and you shall get a sight of the king's son and all the company."

And when the gentles saw the pretty woman that was there they took her to the wedding-room, and they filled for her a glass of wine. She went to drink from it, and a flame went up out of the glass, and a golden pigeon and a silver pigeon sprang out also. They were flying about in the wedding-room when three grains of barley fell on the floor.

The silver pigeon ate the barley; and the golden pigeon said, "Gog, Gog, if you had mind when I cleansed the byre, you would not eat that without giving me a share."

Again fell three other grains of barley, and the silver pigeon ate that, as before.

The golden pigeon said, "Gog, Gog, if you had mind when I thatched the byre, you would not eat that without giving me a share."

Three other grains fell, and still the silver pigeon ate them all.

The golden pigeon said, "Gog, Gog, if you had mind when I harried the magpie's nest, you would not eat that without giving me a share. I lost my finger bringing that down, and I lack it still."

The king's son minded then, and he knew who it was he had got. He sprang where she was, and kissed her from hand to mouth; and so they married a second time. And I left them there.

The GREEN MIST

So you've heard tell of the boggarts, and all the horrid things of old times? You've heard of the voices of dead folks, and hands without arms, that came in the darklins, moaning and crying and beckoning all night through; todloweries dancing on the tussocks, and witches riding on the black snagged roots, that turned to snakes, and raced about with them in the water?

Ay, they were mischancy, unpleasant sort of bodies to do with, and I'm main glad as they were all gone before my days.

Well, in those times folk must have been unlike to now. Instead of doing their work in the week, and smoking their pipes on Sundays, in peace and comfort, they were always bothering their heads about something or other – or the church was doing it for them. The priests were always at them about their souls; and, what with hell and the boggarts, their minds were never easy.

The bogles were once thought a deal more on, and at darklins every night the folk would bear lights in their hands round their houses, saying words to keep them off; and would smear blood on the door sill to scare away the horrors; and would put bread and salt on the flat stones set up by the lane-side to get a good harvest; and would spill water in the four corners of the fields, when they wanted rain; and they thought a deal on the sun, for they reckoned as it made the earth, and brought the good and ill chances and I don't know what all. I reckon they made nigh everything as they saw and heard into great bogles; and they were always giving them things, or saying sort of prayers like, to keep them from doing the folk any evil.

Well, that was a long time ago. So there were, so to say, two churches; one with priests and candles, and all that; the other just a lot of old ways, kept up all unbeknown and hidden-like, mid the folk themselves; and they thought a deal more on the old spells than on the service in the church itself. But as time went on the two got sort of mixed up, and some of the folks couldn't have told you if it were for one or the other as they done the things.

To Yule, in the churches, there were grand services, with candles and flags and what not; and in the cottages there were candles and cakes and grand doings; but the priests never knowed as many of the folks were only waking the dying year, and that the wine teemed upon the door sill to first cock-crow were to bring good luck in the new year. And I reckon as some of the folks themselves would do the old heathen ways and sing hymns meantime, with never a thought of the strangeness of it.

Still, there were many as kept to the old ways altogether, though they did it hidden-like; and I'm going to tell you of one family my grandfather knowed fine, and how they waked the Spring one year.

As I said before, I can't, even if I would, tell you all the things as they used to do; but there was one time of the year as they particularly went in for their spells and prayers, and that was the early Spring. They thought as the earth was sleeping all the Winter; and that the bogles – call them what you will – had nobbut to do but mischief, for they'd nowt to see to in the fields: so they were feared on the long dark Winter days and nights, in the middle of all sorts of unseen fearsome things, ready and waiting for a chance to play them evil tricks.

But as the Winter went by, they thought as it were time to wake the earth from its sleeping and set the bogles to work, caring for the growing things, and bringing the harvest.

After that, the earth were tired, and were sinking to sleep again; and they used to sing hushieby songs in the fields of the Autumn evens.

But in the Spring they went – the folk did as believed in the old ways – to every field in turn, and lifted a spud of earth from the mools; and they said strange and queer words, as they couldn't scarce understand themselves, but the same as had been said for hundreds of years. And every morning at the first dawn, they stood on the door sill, with salt and bread in their hands, watching and waiting for the green mist as rose from the fields and told that the earth were awake again; and the life were coming to the trees and the plants, and the seeds were bursting with the beginning of the Spring.

Well, there was one family as had done all that, year after year, for as long as they knowed of, just as their grandfathers had done it before them; and one Winter they were making ready for waking the Spring.

They had had a lot of trouble through the Winter, sickness and what not had been bad in the place; and the daughter, a ramping young maid, was growed white and waffling like a bag of bones, instead of being the prettiest lass in the village, as she had been before.

Day after day she grew whiter and sillier, till she couldn't stand upon her feet more than a new born babby, and she could only lay at the window, watching and watching the Winter creep away.

And, "Oh, mother," she'd keep saying over and over again, "if I could only wake the Spring with you again, may be the green mist would make me strong and well, like the trees and the flowers and the corn in the fields."

And the mother would comfort her like, and promise that she'd come with them again to the waking, and grow as strong and straight as ever. But day after day she got whiter and wanner, till she looked like a snowflake fading in the sun; and day after day the Winter crept by, and the waking of the Spring was almost there.

The poor maid watched and waited for the time for going to the fields, she had got so weak and sick that she knew she couldn't get there with the rest. But she wouldn't give up, for all that; and her mother must swear that she would lift the lass to the door sill, at the coming of the green mist, so as she might toss out the bread and salt on the earth her own self and with her own poor thin hands.

And still the days went by, and the folk were going on early morns to lift the spud in the fields; and the coming of the green mist was looked for every dawning.

79

The Green Mist

And one even, the lass, as had been laying with her eyes fixed on the little garden, said to her mother, "If the green mist doesn't come in the morn's dawning, I'll not can wait for it longer. The mools is calling me, and the seeds is brusting as will bloom over my head. I know it well, mother. And yet, if I could only see the Spring wake once again – mother – I swear as I'd ask no more than to live as long as one of those cowslips as come every year by the gate, and to die with the first of them when the Summer is in."

The mother whisht the maid in fear; for the bogles and things as they believed in were always gainhand, and could hear owt as was said. They were never safe, never alone, the poor folk to then, with the things as they couldn't see, and couldn't hear, all round them.

But the dawn of the next day brought the green mist. It came from the mools, and happed itself round everything, green as the grass in Summer sunshine, and sweet-smelling as the herbs of the Spring. And the lass was carried to the door sill, where she crumbled the bread and salt on to the earth with her own hands, and said the strange old words of welcoming to the new Spring.

And she looked to the gate, where the cowslips grew, and then she was taken back to her bed by the window, when she slept like a babby, and dreamt of Summer and flowers and happiness.

Whether it was the green mist as done it, I can't tell you, but from that day she grew stronger and prettier than ever, and by the time the cowslips were budding she was running about and laughing like a very sunbeam in the old cottage. But she was always so white and wan, while she looked like a will-o-the-wyke flitting about; and on the cold days she'd sit shaking over the fire and look nigh dead, but when the sun came out, she'd dance and sing in the light, and stretch out her arms to it, as if she only lived by the warmness of it.

And by and by the cowslips burst their buds, and came in flower, and the maid was grown so strange and beautiful that they were nigh feared on her – and every morning she would kneel by the cowslips and water and tend them and dance to them in the sunshine, while her mother would stand begging her to leave them, and cried that

The Green Mist

she would have them pulled up by the roots and throwed away. But the lass only looked strange at her, and said — soft and low like:

"If you aren't tired of me, mother – never pick one of them flowers: they'll fade of their selves soon enough; ay, soon enough, you know."

And the mother would go back to the cottage and greet over the work. But she never said nowt of her trouble to the neighbours – not till afterwards.

But one day a lad of the village stopped at the gate to chat with them, and by and by, whiles he was gossiping, he picked a cowslip and played with it. The lass didn't see what he had done; but as he said goodbye he gave it to her, smiling like, and thinking what a pretty maid it was.

She looked at the flower and at the lad, and all round about her; at the green trees, and the sprouting grass, and the yellow blossoms; and up at the golden shining sun itelf; and all to once, shrinking as if the light she had loved so much were burning her, she ran into the house, without a spoken word, only a sort of cry, like a dumb beast in pain, and the cowslip catched close against her breast.

And then she never spoke again; but lay on the bed, staring at the flower in her hand and fading as it faded all through the day. And at the dawning there was only lying on the bed a wrinkled, white, shrunken dead thing, with in its hand a shrivelled cowslip. And the mother covered it over with the clothes and thought of the beautiful joyful maid dancing like a bird in the sunshine by the golden nodding blossoms, only the day gone by.

The bogles had heard her and given her the wish. She had bloomed with the cowslips, and had faded with the first of them. It's as true as death.

The ROSE TREE

here was once a good man who had two children, a girl by a first wife, a boy by a second. The girl was as white as milk, and her lips were like cherries. Her hair was like golden silk, and it hung to the ground. Her brother loved her dearly, but her wicked stepmother hated her.

"Child," said the stepmother one day, "go to the grocer and buy me a pound of candles." She gave her the money; and the girl went, bought the candles, and started back home. There was a stile to cross. She put down the candles whilst she got over the stile. Up came a dog and ran off with the candles.

She went back to the grocer, and she got a second bunch. She came to the stile, and put down the candles whilst she got over. Up came the dog and ran off with the candles.

She went again to the grocer, and she got a third bunch. She came to the stile, and put down the candles whilst she got over. Up came the dog and ran off with the candles. Then she came to her stepmother crying, for she had spent all the money and had lost three bunches of candles.

The stepmother said to the child, "Come, lay your head on my lap that I may comb your hair." So the girl laid her head in the woman's lap, who began to comb the yellow silken hair. And when she combed, the hair fell over her knees, and rolled right down to the ground.

Then the stepmother hated her more for the beauty of her hair; so she said to her, "I cannot part your hair on my knee, fetch a billet of wood." So she fetched it. Then the stepmother said, "I cannot part your hair with a comb, fetch me an axe." So she fetched it.

"Now," said the wicked woman, "lay your head down on the billet whilst I part your hair."

Well, she laid down her golden head without fear; and whist! down came the axe, and the head was off. So the mother wiped the axe and laughed.

Then she took the heart and liver of the girl, and she stewed them and brought them into the house for supper. The man tasted them, and shook his head. She gave some to the boy, but he would not eat. She tried to make him, but he ran into the garden, and took up his sister, and buried her under a rose tree; and every day he went to the tree and wept, and his tears sank into the ground.

One day, the rose tree flowered; and among the flowers was a white bird; and it sang, and sang, and sang. Then away it flew, and it went to a cobbler, and perched itself on a tree hard by, and sang:

> "My wicked mother slew me,
> My dear father ate me,
> My little brother whom I love
> Sits below, and I sing above
> Stick, stock, stone dead."

"Sing again, sweet bird, the beautiful song," said the cobbler.

"First give me the red shoes you are making," said the bird.

The cobbler gave the shoes, and the bird sang the song. Then away it flew, and it went to a watchmaker, and perched itself on a tree hard by, and sang:

> "My wicked mother slew me,
> My dear father ate me,
> My little brother whom I love
> Sits below, and I sing above
> Stick, stock, stone dead."

"Oh, the beautiful song! Sing it again, sweet bird!" said the watchmaker.

"First give me the gold watch and chain you are making," said the bird.

The watchmaker gave the gold watch and chain, and the bird sang the song. Then away it flew, and it went to where three millers were picking a millstone, and perched itself on a tree hard by, and sang:

> "My wicked mother slew me,
> My dear father ate me,
> My little brother whom I love
> Sits below, and I sing above
> Stick!"

Then one of the millers put down his pick and looked up from his work.
"Stock!"

Then the second miller put down his pick and looked up.
"Stone!"

Then the third miller put down his pick and looked up.
"Dead!"

Then all three millers cried out, "Oh, the song! The beautiful song! Sweet bird, sing it again!"

"First put the millstone you are picking around my neck," said the bird.

The millers did so, and the bird sang the song. Then away it flew, with the millstone, the gold watch and the chain and the red shoes, all the way home.

The bird rattled the millstone against the eaves of the house, and the stepmother said, "It thunders." Then the boy ran out to see the thunder, and down dropped the red shoes at his feet.

The bird rattled the millstone against the eaves of the house once more, and the stepmother said again, "It thunders." Then the father ran out, and down fell the gold watch and chain about his neck.

In ran father and son, laughing, and saying, "See what the thunder has brought us!" Then the bird rattled the millstone against the eaves of the house a third time; and the stepmother said, "It thunders again. Perhaps the thunder has brought something for me," and she ran out; but the moment she went over the doorsill, down fell the millstone on her; and so she died.

The Little Fox

n old former times, when there used to be kings and queens, there was a king and queen who had only one daughter. And they stored this daughter like the eyes in their head, and they hardly would let the wind blow on her. They lived in a tremendous big park, and at one end of the park was a lodge-house, and at the other end there was a great moat of water.

Now this queen died and left this daughter, and she was a very handsome girl – she must have been, being a queen's daughter.

In this here lodge-house there was an old woman lived, (and in them days there was witchcraft), and the old king used to send for her to go up to the palace to work.

So one day this here old gentleman, the king, was talking to this old woman, the witch, and the daughter got a bit jealous; and this old woman found out that the daughter was angry, and so she didn't come near the house for a long time.

Now the old witch was learning the young lady to sew. So she sent for her to come down to the lodge-house before she had her breakfast. And the first day she went, she picked up a kernel of wheat as she was coming along, and ate it.

And the witch said to her, "Have you had your breakfast?"

And she says, "No."

"Have you had nothing?" says the witch.

"No," she says, "only a kernel of wheat."

She went two mornings like that, and picked up a kernel of wheat every morning, so that the witch would have no power over her. But the third morning she picked up only a bit of apple peel; and then this old wise woman witchered her, and after that she never sent for her to come no more.

Now this young lady got to be big. And the witch was glad. She went to the king, and she says, "Your daughter is that way. She's going to have a child. Now you know she'll have to be destroyed."

"What!" says the king. "My beautiful handsome daughter to be in that way! Oh no, no, no, it couldn't be!"

"But it can be so, and it is so," says the old witch.

Well, it was so; and the old king found it out and was well-nigh crazy. And when he found it out, for sure, them days, when any young woman had a misfortune, she used to be burnt. And he ordered a man to go and get an iron chair and a cartload of faggots; and she had to be put in this iron chair, and these faggots set of a light round her, and she had to be burnt to death.

As they had her in this chair, and were going to set it of a light, there was an old gentleman come up, and he says, "My noble liege, don't burn her, nor don't hurt her, nor don't destroy her; for there's an old vessel in the bottom of that park, on the moat. Put her in there, and let her go where she will."

So they did so, and never thought no more about her.

During time this young lady was confined of a little fox. And directly he was born, he says, "My mammy, you must be very weak and low being confined of me, and nothing to eat or drink; but I must go somewheres, and get you something."

"Oh, my dear little fox," says she, "don't leave me. Whatever shall I do without you? I shall die broken-hearted."

"I'm going to my grandfather, as I suppose," says the little fox.

"My dear, you mustn't go; you'll be worried by the dogs."

"Oh! No dogs won't hurt me, my mammy."

Away he went, tritting and trotting till he got to his grandfather's hall. When he got up to the great boarden gates, they were closed, and there were two or three dogs tied down; and when he went in, the dogs never looked at him. One of the women came out of the hall, and who should it be but this old witch!

He says, "Call your dogs in, missis, and don't let them bite me. I want to see the noble liege belonging to this hall."

"What do you want to see him for?"

"I want to see him for something to eat and drink for my mammy, she's very poorly."

"And who is your mammy?"

"Let him come out, he'll know."

So the noble liege came out, and he says, "What do you want, my little fox?"

"I want something to eat and drink for my mammy, she's very poorly."

So the noble liege told the cook to fill a basket with wine and vittles. The cook did so, and brought it to him.

The noble liege says, "My little fox, you can never carry it. I will send someone to carry it."

But he says, "No, thank you, my noble liege." And he chucked it on his little back, and went tritting and trotting to his mammy.

When he got to his mammy, she says, "Oh, my dear little fox, I thought the dogs had eaten you."

"No, my mammy, they turned their heads the other way."

And she took him and kissed him and rejoiced over him.

"Now, my mammy, have something to eat and drink," says the little fox. "I got them from my grandfather, as I suppose it is."

So he went three times. And the second time he went, the old witch became suspicious, and she says to the servants, "Don't let little fox come here no more."

But he says, "I want to see the noble liege," says the little fox.

"You're very plaguesome to the noble liege, my little fox," says the witch.

"Oh no I'm not," he says.

The last time he comes, his mother dressed him in a beautiful robe of fine needlework. Now the noble liege comes up again to the little fox, and he says, "Who is your mammy, my little fox?"

"You wouldn't know perhaps if I was to tell you."

And he says, "Who made you that robe, my little fox?"

"My mammy, to be sure! Who else should make it?"

And the old king wept and cried bitterly when he saw this robe he had on, for he thought his dear child was dead.

"Could I have a word with you, my noble liege?" says the little fox. "Could you call a party this afternoon up at your hall?"

He says, "What for, my little fox?"

"Well, if you call a party, I'll tell you whose robe that is, but you must let my mammy come as well."

"No, no, my little fox; I couldn't have your mammy to come."

Well, the old king agreed, and the little fox says, "Now there must be tales to be told, and songs to be sung, and them as don't sing a song has to tell a tale. And after we have dinner let's go and walk about in the garden. But you must acquaint as many ladies and gentlemen as you can to this party, and be sure to bring the old lady that lives at the lodge."

Well, this party was called, and they all had enough to eat; and after that was over, the noble liege stood up in the middle and called for a song or tale. There were all songs sung and tales told, till it came to this young lady's turn; and she says, "I can't sing a song or tell a tale, but my little fox can."

"Pooydorda!" says the old witch. "Turn out the little fox, he stinks."

But they all called on the little fox, and he stood up and says, "Once on a time," he says, "there was an oldfashioned king and queen lived together; and they only had one daughter, and they stored this daughter like the eyes in their head, and they hardly would let the wind blow on her."

"Pooydorda!" says the old witch. "Turn out the little fox, he stinks."

But there were all the ladies and gentlemen clapping and saying, "Speak on, my little fox!" "Well told, my little fox!" "Very good tale indeed!"

So the little fox spoke on, and told them all about the old witch, and how she wanted to destroy the king's daughter, and he says, "This here old lady, she fried my mammy an egg and a slice of bacon; and if she was to eat it all, she'd be in the family way with some bad animal; but she only ate half of it, and then she was with me. And that's the old witch there," he says, showing the party with his little paw.

And then, after this was done, and they all walked together in the garden, the little fox says, "Now, my mammy, I've done all the good I can for you, and now I'm going to leave you." And he stripped off his little skin, and he flew away.

And the old witch was burnt in the same chair that was meant for the young lady.

The OLD WITCH

nℯ upon a time there were two girls who lived
'heir father and mother. Their father had no
work, and ⸱' ⸱ to go away and seek their fortunes.

Noⱱ to service, and her mother said she might,
if ⸱' started for the town. Well, she went all
d a girl like her. So she went on farther
⸱ to a place where there was an oven where
⸱aking.

⸱⸱⸱, "Little girl, little girl, take us out, take us out.
⸱ we been baking, and no one has come to take us out."
⸱⸱ took the bread out, laid it on the ground, and went on her

ⱱ

'⸱ hen she met a cow, and the cow said, "Little girl, little girl, milk me,
milk me. Seven years have I been waiting, and no one has come to milk
me."

The girl milked the cow into the pails that stood by.

Then she went on farther, and came to an apple tree, so loaded with
fruit that its branches were breaking, and the tree said, "Little girl, little
girl, help me, help me. My branches are breaking, my fruit is so heavy."

And the girl said, "Of course I will, you poor tree." So she shook the
fruit all off, propped up the branches, and left the fruit on the ground
under the tree. Then she went on again till she came to a house.

Now in this house there lived a witch, and this witch took girls into
her house as servants. And when she heard that this girl had left home to
seek service, she said that she would try her, and give her good wages.

The witch told the girl what work she was to do. "You must keep the
house clean and tidy, sweep the floor and the fireplace; but there is one
thing you must never do. You must never look up the chimney, or
something bad will befall you."

The Old Witch

So the girl promised to do as she was told; but one morning, as she was cleaning, and the witch was out, she forgot what the witch had said, and she looked up the chimney. When she did this, a great bag of money fell down in her lap. This happened again and again, each time she looked; so the girl started to go off home.

When she had gone some way, she heard the witch coming after her. So she ran to the apple tree, and cried:

> "Apple tree, apple tree, hide me,
> So the old witch can't find me;
> If she does, she'll break my bones,
> And bury me under the marble stones."

So the apple tree hid her. The witch came up, and said:

> "Tree of mine, tree of mine,
> Have you seen a girl
> With a willy-willy wag, and a long-tailed bag,
> Who's stole my money, all I had?"

And the apple tree said, "No, mother; not for seven year."

When the witch had gone down another way, the girl went on again, and just as she got to the cow she heard the witch coming after her again. So she ran to the cow, and cried:

> "Cow, cow, hide me,
> So the old witch can't find me;
> If she does, she'll break my bones,
> And bury me under the marble stones."

So the cow hid her.

When the witch came up, she looked about and said to the cow:

> "Cow of mine, cow of mine,
> Have you seen a girl
> With a willy-willy wag, and a long-tailed bag,
> Who's stole my money, all I had?"

The Old Witch

And the cow said, "No, mother; not for seven year."

When the witch had gone down another way, the girl went on again, and when she was near the oven she heard the witch coming after her again. So she ran to the oven, and cried:

> "Oven, oven, hide me,
> So the old witch can't find me;
> If she does, she'll break my bones,
> And bury me under the marble stones."

And the oven said, "I've no room. Ask the baker." And the baker hid her behind the oven.

When the witch came up, she looked here and there and everywhere, and then said to the baker:

> "Man of mine, man of mine,
> Have you seen a girl
> With a willy-willy wag, and a long-tailed bag,
> Who's stole my money, all I had?"

And the baker said, "Look in the oven."

The old witch went to look, and the oven said, "Get in and look." The witch got in, and when she was inside, the oven shut the door.

The girl then went off again, and reached her home with the money bags, married a rich man, and lived happy ever after.

So the other sister thought she would go and do the same. And she went along the same way. But when she reached the oven, and the bread said, "Little girl, little girl, take us out, take us out. Seven years have we been baking, and no one has come to take us out," the girl said, "No. I don't want to burn my fingers."

So she went on till she met the cow, and the cow said, "Little girl, little girl, milk me, milk me. Seven years have I been waiting, and no one has come to milk me."

But the girl said, "No. I can't milk you. I'm in a hurry," and went on faster.

Then she came to the apple tree, and the apple tree said, "Little girl, little girl, help me, help me. My branches are breaking, my fruit is so heavy."

But the girl said, "No. I can't shake your fruit. Another day perhaps I may," and went on till she came to the witch's house.

Well, it happened to her just the same as to the other girl: she forgot what she was told, and, one day when the witch was out, she looked up the chimney, and down fell a bag of money. Well, she thought she would be off at once. When she reached the apple tree, she heard the witch coming after her, and she cried:

> "Apple tree, apple tree, hide me,
> So the old witch can't find me;
> If she does, she'll break my bones,
> And bury me under the marble stones."

But the tree did not answer; and she ran on further.
Presently the witch came up, and said:

> "Tree of mine, tree of mine,
> Have you seen a girl
> With a willy-willy wag, and a long-tailed bag,
> Who's stole my money, all I had?"

The tree said, "Yes, mother; she's gone down that way."

So the old witch went after her; and found her; and broke her bones; and buried her under the marble stones.

The
SEAWIFE
and the
CRONE

here was before now a poor old fisher, but he was not getting much fish. There rose a seawife at the side of his boat, and she said, "Well, Duncan, are you getting fish?"

"No," said he. "I am getting no fish at all."

"What will you give me," said the seawife, "if I send you plenty of fish?"

"Well then," said he, "I have but little to give."

"Will you give me the first son that you have?" said the seawife.

"I would give you that, if I were to have a son; there was not, and there will not be, a son of mine," said the old man. "I and my wife are grown so old."

"Name all you have," said the seawife.

"I have but an old mare of a horse, an old dog, myself and my wife. Those are all the creatures of the great world that are mine," said he.

"Here, then," said the seawife, "are three grains for you that you shall give to your wife this very night, and three others to the dog, and these three to the mare, and these three likewise you shall plant behind your house; and in their own time your wife shall have three sons, the mare three foals, and the dog three pups, and there will grow three trees behind your house: and the trees will be a sign; when one of the sons dies, one of the trees will wither. Now, take yourself home, and remember me when your first son is three years of age; and you yourself will get plenty of fish after this."

Everything happened as the seawife said, and the old man got plenty of fish; but when the end of the time was nearing, he grew sorrowful, heavy hearted, while he failed each day as it came. On the namesake of the day, he went to fish; but he did not take his son with him.

The seawife rose at the side of the boat, and said, "Did you bring your son with you here to me?"

"Ach! I did not bring him," said the old man. "I forgot that this was the day."

"Yes, yes! Then," said the seawife, "you shall get four other years of him, to try if it will be easier for you to part from him."

The fisher went home full of glee and delight that he had got four other years of his son, and he kept on fishing, and getting plenty of fish; but at the end of the four years sorrow and woe struck him, and he took not a meal, and he did not a turn, and his wife could not think what was ailing him.

This time he did not know what to do, but he set it before him that he would not take his son. He went to fish; and the seawife rose at the side of the boat, and she asked him, "Did you bring your son here to me?"

"Ach!" said the old man, "I forgot him this time, too."

"Go home, then," said the seawife, "and at the end of seven years after this you are sure to remember me; but then it will not be the easier for you to part with him, but you shall get fish."

The old man went home full of joy; he had got seven other years of his son, and before seven years passed, the old man thought, he himself would be dead, and he would meet the seawife no more.

But when the end of those seven years was nearing, the old man was not without care and trouble. He had rest neither day nor night.

The eldest son asked his father one day if anyone was besetting him. The old man said that someone was, but that belonged neither to his son nor to anybody else. The lad said that he had to know what it was. His father told him at last how the matter lay between him and the seawife.

"Let that not put you in any trouble," said the son; "I shall go to her."

"You shall not; you shall not go, my son," said the old man, "even though I should not get fish for ever."

"If you will not let me," said the son, "go to the smithy, and have the smith make me a great strong sword, and I shall go to the end of fortune."

His father went to the smithy, and the smith made the sword for him. The lad grasped it and gave it a shake or two, and it went in a hundred splinters. He asked his father to go to the smithy and get him another sword of twice the weight; and his father did so, and so likewise it happened to that next sword: it broke in two halves.

Back went the old man to the smithy; and the smith made a great sword: its like he never made before.

"There's your sword for you," said the smith, "and the fist must be good that plays this blade."

Then the old man gave the sword to his son, and he brandished it a shake or two. "This is the sword," said he. "I shall go where there is not a drop of salt water."

The next morning he put a saddle on the black horse that the mare had, and he put the world under his head, and the black dog was by his side.

When he had gone on a bit, he found the carcass of a sheep beside the road; and at the carrion were a wolf, a falcon and an otter. He came down off the horse, and he divided the carcass amongst the three: three shares to the wolf, two shares to the otter, and a share to the falcon.

"For this," said the wolf, "if swiftness of foot or sharpness of tooth will aid you, remember me, and I shall be at your side."

Said the otter, "If the swimming of foot on the ground of a pool will aid you, remember me, and I shall be at your side."

And the falcon said, "If hardship comes on you, where swiftness of wing or crook of a claw will aid you, remember me, and I shall be at your side."

The lad went from there till he reached a king's house, and he took service as a cowherd, and his wages were to be according to the milk of the cattle. He went away with the cattle, and the grazing was only bare; and when he took them home they had not much milk, and his meat and drink were poor that night.

The next day, he went on further with the cattle; and at last he came to a place exceedingly grassy, in a green glen, of which he never saw the like.

But about the time when he should walk behind the cattle for taking them homewards, he heard a noise: "Firum Farum", little stones going under, "Firum Farum", great gravel going over; and he saw a giant coming with a sword in his hand.

"Hiu! Hau! Hogaraich!" said the giant. "It is long since my teeth rusted seeking your flesh. The cattle are mine; they are on my march; and a dead man are you."

"That may be easier to say than to do," said the lad.

To grips they go: himself and the giant. He drew the great clean-sweeping sword, and in the play of the battle the black dog leaped on the giant's back. The lad swung his sword, and the head was off the giant in a twinkling.

The lad leaped on the black horse, and he went to look for the giant's house. He reached a door, and in the haste that the giant had made he had left each gate and door open. There was magnificence and money in plenty, but the lad took not a thing from the giant's house. And when the cattle were milked that night, there was a flood of milk, and the king had to send for carpenters to make milkpails: such milk had never been seen in the king's dairy. And the lad got good feeding, meat and drink without stint.

The lad went on for a time in this way, but at last the glen grew bare of grass, and the grazing was not so good. But he thought he would go a little further forward in on the giant's land; he saw a great park of grass. He went back for the cattle, and he put them into the park.

They were but a short time grazing in the park when the lad heard a greater and louder clatter than ever: "Firum Farum", little stones going under, "Firum Farum", great gravel going over; and he saw a wild giant coming, full of rage and madness.

"Hiu! Hau! Hogaraich!" said the giant. "A drink of your blood shall quench my thirst tonight."

"That is easier to say than to do," said the lad.

And at each other they went. At length and at last it seemed as if the giant would get the victory over the lad; but he called on his dog, and with one spring the dog caught the giant by the neck, and the lad struck off the head.

He went home very tired that night, but the king's cattle had the milk.

He followed herding in this way for a time; but one night after he came home, instead of getting hello and good luck from the dairymaid, all the house was at crying and woe. He asked what was the cause. The dairymaid said that a waterbeast with three heads was in the loch, and the waterbeast was to get feeding of flesh, and man-flesh, every year, and the choice had come on the king's daughter that year. "And in the morning," said the dairymaid, "she is to meet the waterbeast; but there is a suitor yonder who is going to save her."

"What suitor is that?" said the lad.

"Oh," said the dairymaid, "he is a cock-eyed carroty-headed cook; and when he kills the waterbeast he will marry the king's daughter, for the king has said that he who could save his daughter should get her for marrying."

But in the morning, when the time was near, the king's daughter and the cock-eyed, carroty-headed cook went to meet the waterbeast; and they reached the black corrie at the upper end of the loch. They were but a little time there when the waterbeast stirred in the middle of the loch; and the cock-eyed, carroty-headed cook, seeing this terror with three heads, he took fright, and he slunk away, and he hid himself. And the king's daughter was under fear and trembling, with no one at all to save her.

She looked, and saw the lad coming on his black horse, and his black dog moving after.

"There is gloom on your face, girl," said the lad. "What are you doing here?"

"I shall not be here long," said the king's daughter; "for a waterbeast is coming to take me away."

"I shall stay with you," said the lad, "and keep you company for a while." Then he laid his head in her lap to sleep, and she combed his hair.

"But if you sleep," said the king's daughter, "what will rouse you?"

"Rousing for me," said the lad, "is to put the gold ring that is on your finger on my little finger."

They were not long there when the king's daughter saw a dark squall coming from the west, the loch water running east and the waves waxing, and in the squall the waterbeast blowing spray and spindrift. She took the ring from her finger, and put it on the little finger of the lad. He awoke, and he went to meet the waterbeast with his sword and his dog.

The lad and the waterbeast fell upon each other with rattling of stones and splashing of billows, till, man and dog doing the best they could, the lad swept off one of the waterbeast's heads.

"If I had a draught of fair water," said the beast, "I would tear you to pieces now."

"If I had a draught of red wine," said the lad, "I would kill you today."

"If one head is off, two are on," said the beast, and it drove the loch in foam from end to end, and in a twinkling was gone.

"I am safe for one night," said the king's daughter, "but the beast will come again, and for ever, until the other two heads are off."

The lad caught the waterbeast's head, and he drew a withy through it, and he told the king's daughter to take it with her. She went home with the head on her shoulder, and the lad went to herd the cows.

The king's daughter had not gone far when the cock-eyed, carroty-headed cook saw her, and he said that he would kill her if she did not say that it was he that took the head off the waterbeast.

"Oh," said she, "I shall say it. Who else took the head off the beast but you?"

They reached the king's house, and the head was on the cock-eyed, carroty cook's shoulder. And in the morning they went away again, and there was no question at all but that this hero would save the king's daughter. They reached the same place, and they were not long there when the fearful waterbeast stirred in the middle of the loch, and the cock-eyed, carroty-headed cook slunk away as he had done the day before, and up came the lad on the black horse.

"Come up and take breath," said the king's daughter.

The lad lay down at the side of the king's daughter, and she combed his hair, and he said, "If I sleep before the beast comes, rouse me."

"What is rousing for you?" said she.

"Rousing for me is to put the ring that is in your ear in mine," said the lad.

The lad was not long asleep before the king's daughter saw the west grow dark and the loch run east, and the waves came big and gurly. She cried, "Rouse! Rouse!" but he would not wake; so she took the ring from her ear and put it in his, and at once he was on his feet and down to the loch to meet the waterbeast, and they went to it, spluttering, splashing, raving and roaring, till the lad, just before night, cut off another head.

The lad put the head on a withy, leaped on his horse, and took himself off to the herding. The king's daughter went home, and the cock-eyed, carroty-headed cook came out of a hole where he was hiding and said that he would kill her if she did not say that he was the hero. "Who else but you," said she, "would be the hero?"

If the king was hopeful the first night, he was now sure that the cock-eyed, carroty-headed cook would save his daughter, and there was no question at all but that the waterbeast would be dead in the morning.

The next day the two went together, and the cock-eyed, carroty-headed cook hid in a hole, and the lad came on his horse.

"What is rousing for you this time?" said the king's daughter.

"Rousing for me," said the lad, "is for you to take the other ring from your other ear and to put it in my other ear."

And when the waterbeast came, she put the other ring in his other ear, and he awoke, and at the waterbeast he went; and if roaring and raving, raving and roaring, were on them the other days, then this day it was horrible.

"If I had a draught of water I would win yet," said the beast."

"If I had a draught of wine," said the lad, "I would kill you."

But no matter of that, the king's daughter heard him, and she took wine and ran to the lad, and he drank a draught.

"If two heads are off, one is on," said the beast.

"Better would be three," said the lad, and he swept off the last head; and the beast was a pool of water and a heap of sand.

The lad drew a withy through the last head, and the king's daughter took it home. The cock-eyed, carroty cook came out of the hole, and he was to marry the king's daughter the next day, but that the king said that first he should take the heads off the withy without cutting it. "For," said the king, "who should take the heads off the withy but the man that put the heads on?"

The cock-eyed, carroty cook tried them, but he could not take the heads off; nor could any of the household, though they all tried. The king asked if there was anyone else about the house, and they said that the lad who was cowherd had not tried them yet. The lad was sent for, and he was not long in throwing the heads hither and thither off the withy.

"But stop a bit, my lad," said the king's daughter. "The man that took the heads off the waterbeast, he has the ring from my finger and the rings from my two ears."

The lad put his hand in his pocket, and he threw the rings on the board.

"You are my man," said the king's daughter.

The king was not so pleased, but they were married that same night.

Now they were happy, and everything going on well. And one day they took themselves to the salt shore. But while they were straying and playing amongst the reefs and stones on the ebb, the seawife rose and made a rush and seized the lad and said, "It is many a day since you were promised to me, and now I have you." And then she swallowed him up.

The king's daughter was now mournful, tearful, blind-sorrowful for her married man. An old smith met her, and she told him how it had befallen.

"Go," said the smith, "and take everything you have that is finer than another, and spread them in the very same place where the seawife took away your man."

She did so. The seawife put up her nose from the water and said, "Fine is your jewellery, king's daughter."

"Finer than that is the jewel you took from me," said she. "Give me one sight of my husband, and you shall get any one thing of all that you see."

The seawife put the lad up into her mouth.

"Deliver him to me," said the king's daughter, "and you shall get all that you see."

The seawife put the lad out onto the shore, and then took all the jewels, and took the king's daughter, and left the lad sorrowful, mournful, tearful, wandering down and up about the banks, by day and by night.

The old smith met him. "Well," said the smith, "there is but one way to win back the king's daughter, and to kill the seawife.

"In the middle of the sea there is an island; and in the middle of the island there is the white footed hind of the slenderest legs and the swiftest step. And though she may be caught, there will spring a raven out of her. And though the raven may be caught, there will spring a trout out of her. In the mouth of the trout there is an egg, and in the egg is the breath of the seawife; and if the egg breaks, she is dead."

Now there was no getting to the island, for the seawife would sink each boat and raft that would try. The lad thought that he would leap the water with the black horse; and so he did, and the black dog with one bound after him.

In the middle of the island the lad saw the white footed hind of the slenderest legs and the swiftest step, and he let the black dog after her; but when the black dog was on the one side of the island, the hind was on the other, so fleet was she.

"Oh," said the lad, "I wish the wolf of the carcass of flesh were here."

No sooner did he speak than the wolf was with him, and after the hind the wolf went and was not long in fetching her to the earth; but no sooner did he catch her than a raven sprang out of her.

"Oh," said the lad, "now is the hour of the grey falcon."

And straight away the falcon appeared and was after the raven and was not long in fetching the raven to the earth; but the raven fell, out jumped the trout from her and into the sea.

"Otter," said the lad, "it is time to be with me now."

The otter was with him, and out on the sea he leaped and brought the trout to shore; but an egg fell from the trout's mouth.

The lad sprang and put his foot over the egg; and the seawife let out a roar, and she said, "Do not break the egg, and you shall get all that you ask of me."

"Give me back the king's daughter," said the lad.

In the wink of an eye the king's daughter was by his side. And when he got hold of her hand in both his hands he let his foot down on the egg, and the seawife died, for it was her breath that was in the egg.

They left her there, and they went home, and there was delight and smiling in the king's house that night. The king put great honour on the lad, and he was a great man with the king.

So the lad and his wife were happy, and everything going on well; and they were walking one day, when the lad saw a little black castle over against him, and he asked his wife what castle that might be, and who was living there in it.

"No one goes to that castle," said his wife, "for no one who has gone there has yet come back to tell the tale."

"This very night," said the lad, "I shall see who is living in it."

"Go not, go not," said his wife; "there never went man to this castle that returned."

"Be that as it pleases," said the lad. And he went and took himself to the castle.

When he reached the door, a little flattering crone met him combing her hair. "Where are you from, father of my fondness and mother of my love?" said she. "Come till you tell me your tale, come till I tell you mine." And with many words she wiled him, till in he went. Then she took up her magic club, and hit him over the head, and at once he fell, and was made a pillar of stone.

On this night there was woe in the king's house, and in the morning there was wailing in the fisher's hut. For the tree was seen to wither, and the fisher's middle son said that his brother was dead and that he was going to find him.

He mounted his black horse, and his black dog followed him. His father put a fish bone in his hand, and it grew into a gold-hilted sword that gave him wisdom and learning. Away he went; each road was even, and every path smooth, and the black dog ran the track straight and right to the king's house. There never were created two more alike than he and his brother; and the king's daughter thought that he was her own man.

He did not know how in the world he could manage to keep from his brother's chamber that night. So he told the king's daughter that he had laid a heavy wager that he would not go to bed, but he would sleep on a table in front of the bed. And he did so till morning.

Then he looked out, and he saw the little black castle, and said to the king's daughter, "What is that castle?"

"Did I not tell you that yesterday?" said the king's daughter.

"You did not," said he.

So she told him; and he said that he must go, happen hard or soft as it might.

He went to the little castle of the crone, and just as it befell the eldest brother, so in each way it befell the middle son, and with one blow of her magic club, the crone stretched him beside his brother as a pillar of stone.

The old fisher looked out in the morning, and the leaves had fallen from the middle tree. The youngest brother took his horse and dog and gold-hilted sword that his father gave him with wisdom and learning, and off he set. Each road was even and each path smooth for him, and he ran right and straight to the king's house.

The king's daughter saw him, and she went to meet and welcome and embrace him. "It was enough to stay away the first night," said she, "without staying from me last night again."

"Many a man may have matters of moment with gentlefolks, so that it may not be known when he will come," said he. They went to rest, and he laid a cold sword between them.

In the morning, he saw the castle as his brothers had seen it, and asked what castle that would be.

"Did I not tell you yesterday and the day before?" said she.

"You did not," said he.

She told him again; and he said that he must go, happen hard or soft as it might.

The Seawife and the Crone

He went; and he too saw the flattering crone combing her hair.

"Come up, treasure," said she, "son of the father of my desire, and the mother of my love, till you tell me your news, and I tell you mine."

He had no good notion of her, and he whipped off her head with his sword; but the sword flew out of his hand. And the crone grasped her head with both hands, and put it on her neck as it was before.

The dog sprang on the crone, and she struck the generous dog with the club of magic; and there he lay. But the youngest brother went to grips with the crone, and got a hold of the club, and with one blow to the top of the head she was on earth in the wink of an eye. He went forward, up a little, and saw his two brothers side by side as pillars of stone. He gave a blow to each one with the club, and they were men again.

They took the keys from the crone and searched the castle. They found one room full of gold, and one full of silver. They found a room full of fine clothing, and a room full of saddles, and a room full of bridles, and a room full of men of stone, and a vessel of balm for bringing life again.

They came back to the king's house and to rejoicing. The king was growing old. The eldest son of the fisher took his wife and was crowned king, and the pair of brothers stayed a year and a day in the house, and then the two went on their journey home with the gold and silver of the crone; and if they have not died since then, they are alive this very day.

The Little Bull Calf

enturies of years ago, when all the most part of the country was a wilderness place, there was a boy lived in a poor bit of a poverty house. And this boy's father gave him a dear little bull calf. The boy used to think the world of this bull calf, and his father gave him everything he needed for it.

Afterwards his father died, and his mother got married again; and this was a very vicious stepfather, and he couldn't abide this boy. And at last he said, if the boy brought the bull calf home again, he was going to kill it.

The boy used to go out tending his bull calf every day with barley bread. And after that there was an old man came, and he directed the boy: "You and your bull calf had better go away and seek your fortunes."

So he went on, and he went on, as far as I can tell you tomorrow night, and he went up to a farmhouse and begged a crust of bread; and when he came back he broke it in two, and shared it with his little bull calf.

And he went on to another house, and begged a bit of cheese curd; and when he came back he wanted to share it with his bull calf.

"No," says the calf, "I'm going across this field into the wild wood wilderness country, where there'll be tigers, leopards, wolves, monkeys and a fiery dragon. And I shall kill them every one except the fiery dragon, and he'll kill me."

And the boy did cry; and he says, "Oh, my little bull calf, I hope he won't kill you."

"Yes, he will," the little bull calf says. "And you climb up that tree, and then no one can come near you but the monkeys, and if they come the cheese curd will save you.

"And when I'm killed, the dragon will go away for a bit. And you come down this tree and skin me, and get my biggest gut out, and blow it up, and my gut will kill everything that you hit with it; and when that fiery dragon comes, you hit it with my gut, and then cut its tongue out."

(There were fiery dragons in those days; but it isn't the same world now. The world is turned over since, like you turned it over with a spade.)

Of course the boy did as the bull calf told him, and he climbed up the tree, and the monkeys climbed up the tree to him. And he held the cheese curd in his hand, and he says, "I'll squeeze your heart like this flint stone."

And the monkey cocked his eye, as much as to say, "If you can squeeze a flint stone and make the juice come over of it, you can squeeze me." And he never spoke, for a monkey's cunning, but down he went.

And the bull calf was fighting all these wild things on the ground; and the boy was clapping his hands up the tree and saying, "Go on, my little bull calf! Well fought, my little bull calf!" And he mastered everything barring the fiery dragon. And the fiery dragon killed the bull calf.

The boy came down the tree, and skinned the bull calf, and got the biggest gut out; and then he went on.

He saw a young lady, a king's daughter, staked down by the hair of her head. (They were very savage that time of day, kings to their daughters, if they misbehaved themselves, and she had been put there for the fiery dragon to destroy her.)

And the boy sat down with her several hours, and she says, "Now, my dear little boy, my time is come when I'm going to be worried; and you'd better go."

And he says, "No," he says, "I can master it, and I won't go."

She begged and prayed on him as ever she could to get him away, but he wouldn't go. He could hear this dragon coming far enough, roaring and doing; and it came spitting fire, with a tongue like a great spear; you could hear it roaring for miles; and this place where the king's daughter was staked down was its beat.

When the dragon came, the boy hit the gut about its face till it was dead, but the fiery dragon bit his front finger off him.

The boy cut the fiery dragon's tongue out, and he says to the young lady, "I've done all that I can, and I must leave you." She was sorry when he had to leave her, but she tied a diamond ring into his hair, and said good-bye to him.

Now then, by and by, the old king came up to the very place where his daughter was staked by the hair of her head, lamenting and doing, and expecting to see not a bit of his daughter, but the prints of the place where she had been. And he was surprised.

He says to his daughter, "How come you saved?"

"Why, there was a little boy here and he saved me, daddy."

Then the king untied her, and took her home to the palace, for he was glad, when he got his temper back again.

Well, he put it in all the papers to want to know who saved this girl; and if the right man came, he was to marry her, and have his kingdom and all his estate.

There were gentlemen came from all parts of England, with their front fingers cut off, and all kinds of tongues: foreign tongues, and beasts' tongues, and wild animals' tongues. They cut all sorts of tongues out, and they went round shooting things on purpose, but they never could find a dragon to shoot. There were gentlemen coming every other day with tongues and diamond rings; but when they showed their tongues, they weren't the right ones, and they got turned off.

This ragged boy came up a time or two, very desolated like; and she had her eye on him, the king's daughter, and she looked at the boy, till her father got very angry and turned the boy out.

"Daddy," she says, "I've got a knowledge of that boy."

You may say there were all kinds of kings' sons coming up showing their parcels; and after a time or two this boy came up again, dressed a bit better.

The old king says, "I see you've got an eye on this boy, and if it is to be him, it has to be him."

All the other gentlemen were fit to kill him, and they says, "Pooh! Pooh! Turn that boy out; it can't be him."

But the old king says, "Now, my boy, let's see what you've got."

Well, he showed the diamond ring, with her name into it, and the fiery dragon's tongue. How those gentlemen were mesmerised when he showed his authority! And the king told him, "You shall have my estate, and marry my daughter."

And the boy got married to this here girl, and got all the old king's estate. And then the stepfather came and wanted to own him; but the young king didn't know such a man.

MR· FOX

ady Mary was young, and Lady Mary was fair. She had two brothers, and more lovers than she could count. But of them all, the bravest and most gallant was Mr. Fox.

No one knew who Mr. Fox was; but he was certainly brave, and surely rich, and of all her lovers, Lady Mary cared for him alone. At last it was agreed upon between them that they should be married. Lady Mary asked Mr. Fox where they should live, and he described to her his castle, and where it was; but he did not ask her, or her brothers, to come and see it.

So one day, near the wedding, when her brothers were out, Lady Mary set off for Mr. Fox's castle. And after many searchings she came to it, and a fine strong house it was, with high walls and a deep moat. And when she came up to the gateway she saw written on it:

"Be bold, be bold."

Then, as the gate was open, she went through it, and found no one there. So she went up to the doorway, and over it found written:

"Be bold, be bold, but not too bold."

Still she went on, till she came into the hall, and went up the broad stairs till she came to a door in the gallery, over which was written:

"Be bold, be bold, but not too bold,
Lest that your heart's blood should run cold."

But Lady Mary was a brave one, she was, and she opened the door, and what do you think she saw? Why, bodies and skeletons of beautiful young ladies all stained with blood.

So Lady Mary thought it was high time to get out of that horrid place, and she closed the door, went through the gallery, and was just going down the stairs, and out of the hall, when who should she see through the window but Mr. Fox dragging a beautiful young lady along from the gateway to the door.

Lady Mary rushed downstairs, and hid herself behind a cask, just in time, as Mr. Fox came in with the poor young lady. As he got near Lady Mary, Mr. Fox saw a diamond ring glittering on the finger of the young lady he was dragging, and he tried to pull it off. But it was tightly fixed, and would not come off; so Mr. Fox cursed and swore, and drew his sword, raised it, and brought it down on the hand of the poor lady.

The sword cut off the hand, which jumped up into the air, and fell of all places in the world into Lady Mary's lap. Mr. Fox looked about a bit, but did not look behind the cask, so at last he went on dragging the young lady up the stairs and into the Bloody Chamber.

As soon as she heard him pass through the gallery, Lady Mary crept out of the door, down through the gateway, and ran home.

Now it happened that the very next day the marriage contract of Lady Mary and Mr. Fox was to be signed, and there was a splendid breakfast before that. And when Mr. Fox was seated at table opposite Lady Mary, he looked at her.

"How pale you are this morning, my dear."

"Yes," said she. "I had a bad night's rest last night. I had horrible dreams."

"Dreams go by contraries," said Mr. Fox. "Tell us your dream."

"I dreamed," said Lady Mary, "that I went yesterday to your castle, and I found it in the woods, with high walls, and a deep moat, and over the gateway was written:

'Be bold, be bold.'"

"But it is not so, nor it was not so," said Mr. Fox.

"And when I came to the doorway over it was written:

'Be bold, be bold, but not too bold.'"

"It is not so, nor it was not so," said Mr. Fox.

"And then I went upstairs, and came to a gallery, and at the end of it there was a door, on which was written:

'Be bold, be bold, but not too bold,
Lest that your heart's blood should run cold.'"

"It is not so, nor it was not so," said Mr. Fox.

"And then – and then I opened the door, and the room was filled with bodies and skeletons of poor dead women, all stained with their blood."

"It is not so, nor it was not so. And God forbid it should be so," said Mr. Fox.

"Then I dreamed that I ran along the gallery, and just as I was going down the stairs, I saw you, Mr. Fox, coming up to the hall door, dragging after you a young lady, rich and beautiful."

"It is not so, nor it was not so. And God forbid it should be so," said Mr. Fox.

"I went down the stairs, and hid myself behind a cask, when you, Mr. Fox, came in, dragging the young lady by the arm. And, as you passed me, Mr. Fox, I thought I saw you try and get off her diamond ring, and when you could not, Mr. Fox, it seemed to me in my dream, that you out with your sword and hacked off the poor lady's hand to get the ring."

"It is not so, nor it was not so. And God forbid it should be so," said Mr. Fox.

"But it is so, and it was so. Here's hand and ring I have to show."

And Lady Mary pulled out the lady's hand from her dress, and pointed it straight at Mr. Fox.

At once her brothers drew their swords and cut Mr. Fox into a thousand pieces.

The Paddo

poor widow was one day baking bannocks, and she sent her daughter with a dish to the well to bring water. The daughter went, and better went, till she came to the well, but it was dry, and she could not reach the water. Now, what to do she did not know, for she could not go back to her mother without water; she sat down by the side of the well, and fell a-greeting.

A paddo then came loup-loup-louping out of the well, and said, "What for are you greeting, hinny?"

"I cannot reach the water," said she.

"But," said the paddo, "if you'll be my wife, I'll give you plenty of water."

And the girl, not thinking that the poor beast could mean anything serious, said she would be his wife, for the sake of getting the water.

So she got the water into her dish, and went away home to her mother, and thought no more about the paddo, till that night, when, just as she and her mother were about to go to their beds, something came to the door; and when they listened, they heard this song:

> "O open the door, my hinny, my heart,
> O open the door, my own darling;
> Remember the promise that you and I made,
> Down in the meadow, where we two met."

Says the mother to the daughter, "What noise is that at the door?"

"Hout," says the daughter, "it's nothing but a filthy paddo."

"Open the door," says the mother, "to the poor paddo."

So the daughter opened the door, and the paddo came loup-loup-louping in, and sat down by the ingle-side. Then he sings:

The Paddo

"O give me my supper, my hinny, my heart,
O give me my supper, my own darling;
Remember the promise that you and I made,
Down in the meadow, where we two met."

"Hout," says the daughter, "would I give a filthy paddo his supper?"
"O ay," says the mother, "give the poor paddo his supper."
So the paddo got his supper; and after that he sings again:

"O put me to bed, my hinny, my heart,
O put me to bed, my own darling;
Remember the promise that you and I made,
Down in the meadow, where we two met."

"Hout," says the daughter, "would I put a filthy paddo to bed?"
"O ay," says the mother, "put the poor paddo to bed."
And so the daughter put the paddo to bed; and then the paddo sings:

"O give me your kiss, my hinny, my heart,
O give me your kiss, my own darling;
Remember the promise that you and I made,
Down in the meadow, where we two met."

"Hout," says the daughter, "would I give a filthy paddo my kiss?"
"O ay," says the mother, "give the poor paddo your kiss."
And so the daughter gave the paddo her kiss; and then the paddo sings:

"O cuddle my back, my hinny, my heart,
O cuddle my back, my own darling;
Remember the promise that you and I made,
Down in the meadow, where we two met."

"Hout," says the daughter, "would I cuddle the back of a filthy paddo?"
"O ay," says the mother, "cuddle the poor paddo's back."

The Paddo

And so the daughter cuddled the paddo's back; and then the paddo sings again:

> "Now fetch me an axe, my hinny, my heart,
> Now fetch me an axe, my own darling;
> Remember the promise that you and I made,
> Down in the meadow, where we two met."

The daughter wasn't long in fetching the axe; and then the paddo sings:

> "Now chop off my head, my hinny, my heart,
> Now chop off my head, my own darling;
> Remember the promise that you and I made,
> Down in the meadow, where we two met."

Well, the daughter chopped off his head; and no sooner was that done, than he started up, the bonniest young prince in the world. And the two lived happy all the rest of their days. So you see.

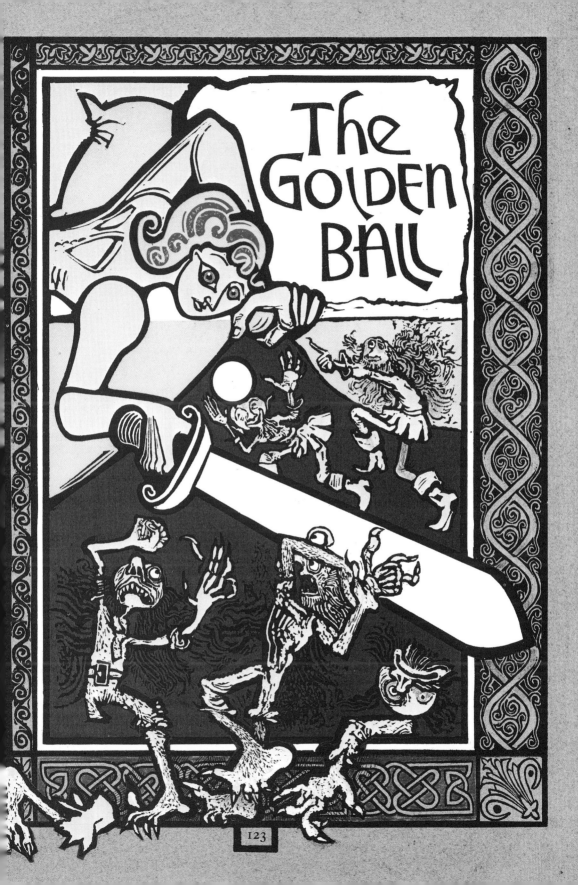

THE GOLDEN BALL

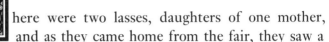here were two lasses, daughters of one mother, and as they came home from the fair, they saw a right bonny young man stand at the house door before them. They had never seen such a bonny chap. He had gold on the cap, gold on the finger, gold on the neck, a red gold watch chain – eh, but he had brass!

He had a golden ball in each hand. He gave a ball to each lass, and she was to keep it; and if she lost it, she was to be hanged.

Well, one of the lasses, it was the youngest, she lost her ball. I'll tell you how. She was by a park paling, and she was tossing her ball, and it went up, and up, and up, till it went fair over the paling; and when she climbed up to look, the ball ran along green grass, and it went right forward to the door of the house that was in the park, and the ball went in and she saw it no more.

So she was taken away to be hanged, because she had lost the ball.

But the lass had a sweetheart, and he said he would get the ball. So he went to the park gate, but it was shut; so he climbed the hedge, and when he got to the top of the hedge, an old woman rose up out of the dyke before him, and said, if he would get the ball, he must sleep three nights in the house. He said he would.

Then he went into the house, and looked for the ball, but could not find it. Night came on, and he heard boggarts move in the courtyard; so he looked out of the window, and the yard was full of them, like maggots in rotten meat.

Presently he heard steps coming upstairs. He hid behind the door, and was as still as a mouse. Then in came a big giant, five times as tall as he was, and the giant looked round but did not see the lad, so he went to the window and bowed to look out; and as he bowed on his elbows to see the boggarts in the yard, the lad stepped behind him, and with one blow of his sword he cut him in two, so that the top part of him fell in the yard, and the bottom part stood looking out of the window.

There was a great cry from the boggarts when they saw half the giant come tumbling down to them, and they called out, "There comes half our master! Give us the other half!"

So the lad said, "It's no use of you, you pair of legs, standing alone at the window, as you have no eyes to see with, so go join your brother." And he cast the bottom part of the giant after the top part. Now when the boggarts had gotten all the giant they were quiet.

Next night the lad was at the house again, and now a second giant came in at the door, and as he came in the lad cut him in two; but the legs walked on to the chimney and went up it. "Go, get you after your legs," said the lad to the head, and he cast the head up the chimney, too.

The third night, the lad got into bed, and he heard the boggarts striving under the bed, and they had the golden ball there, and they were casting it to and fro.

Now one of them has his leg thrussen out from under the bed, so the lad brings his sword down and cuts it off. Then another thrusts his arm out at the other side of the bed, and the lad cuts that off. So at last he had reckoned them all, and they all went off crying and wailing, and forgot the golden ball; but the lad took it from under the bed, and went to seek his truelove.

Now the lass was taken to York to be hanged. She was brought out on the scaffold, and the hangman said, "Now, lass, you must hang by the neck." But she cried out: "Stop, stop, I think I see my mother coming!

> Oh, mother, hast brought my golden ball
>   And come to set me free?"

> "I've neither brought thy golden ball
>   Nor come to set thee free;
> But I have come to see thee hung
>   Upon this gallows-tree."

Then the hangman said, "Now, lass, you must put your head into the noose." But she cried out: "Stop, stop, I think I see my father coming!

The Golden Ball

Oh, father, hast brought my golden ball
    And come to set me free?"

"I've neither brought thy golden ball
    Nor come to set thee free;
But I have come to see thee hung
    Upon this gallows-tree."

Then the hangman said, "Now, lass, you must die." But she cried out: "Stop, stop, I think I see my sisters coming!

Oh, sisters, have you brought my golden ball
    And come to set me free?"

"We've neither brought thy golden ball
    Nor come to set thee free;
But we have come to see thee hung
    Upon this gallows-tree."

Then the hangman said, "Now, lass, I won't stop no longer; you are making game of me. You must hang at once." But now she saw her sweetheart coming, and he had over head in the air her own golden ball; so she cried out: "Stop, stop, I see my sweetheart coming!

Oh, sweetheart, hast brought my golden ball
    And come to set me free?"

"Yes, I have brought thy golden ball
    And come to set thee free;
I have not come to see thee hung
    Upon this gallows-tree."

Then the lad took her down, and of course they were married straight away.

The BLACK HORSE

nce there was a king and he had three sons, and when the king died they did not give a shade of anything to the youngest son but an old white limping garron.

"If I get but this," said the youngest son, "it seems that I had best go with it."

He was going with it right before him, sometimes walking, sometimes riding. When he had been riding a good while he thought that the garron would need a while of eating, so he came down to earth, and what should he see coming out of the heart of the west towards him but a rider riding high, well, and right well.

"All hail, my lad," said the king's son.

"Hail, king's son," said the other.

"What's your news?" said the king's son.

"I have got that," said the lad who came. "I have broken my heart riding this ass of a horse; but will you give me the limping white garron for him?"

"No," said the king's son; "it would be a bad business for me."

"You need not fear," said the lad who came, "there is no saying but that you might make better use of him than I. He has one value: there is no single place that you can think of in the four parts of the wheel of the world that the black horse will not take you there."

So the king's son got the black horse, and he gave the limping white garron.

Where should he think of being when he mounted but in the Land Underwaves. He went, and before sunrise on the morrow he was there. What should he find when he got there but the son of the king of the Land Underwaves holding a court, and the people of the realm gathered to see if there was anyone who would undertake to go to seek the daughter of the king of Norroway to be the prince's wife. No one came forward, when who should come up but the rider of the black horse.

"You, rider of the black horse," said the prince, "I lay you under crosses and under spells to have the daughter of the king of Norroway here before the sun rises tomorrow."

The king's son went out and he reached the black horse and leaned his elbow on his mane, and he heaved a sigh.

"Sigh of a king's son under spells!" said the horse. "But have no care; we shall do the thing that was set before you." And so off they went.

"Now," said the horse, "when we get near the great town of Norroway, you will notice that the four feet of a horse never went to the town before. The king's daughter will see me from the top of the castle looking out, as she will, from a window; and she will not be content without a turn of a ride upon me. Say that she may have that, but the horse will suffer no man but you to ride before a woman on him."

They came near the big town, and the king's son fell to horseman-ship; and the princess was looking out of the windows, and saw the horse. The horseman pleased her, and she came out just as the horse had come.

"Give me a ride on the horse," said she.

"You shall have that," said the king's son, "but the horse will let no man ride him before a woman but me."

"I have a horseman of my own," said she.

"If so, set him in front," said he.

Before the horseman mounted at all, when he tried to get up, the horse lifted his legs and kicked him off.

"Come then yourself and mount before me," said she. "I won't leave the matter so."

He mounted the horse and she behind him, and before she glanced from her she was nearer sky than earth. He was in the Land Underwaves with her before sunrise.

"You are come," said the prince of the Land Underwaves.

"I am come," said he.

"There you are, my hero," said the prince. "You are the son of a king, but I am a son of success. Anyhow, we shall have no delay or neglect now, but a wedding.''

"Just gently," said the princess of Norroway. "Your wedding is not so short a way off as you suppose. Till I get the silver cup that my grandmother had at her wedding, and that my mother had as well, I will not marry, for I need to have it at my own wedding."

"You, rider of the black horse," said the prince of the Land Underwaves, "I set you under spells and under crosses unless the silver cup is here before dawn tomorrow."

Out he went, the king's son, and reached the horse and leaned his elbow on his mane, and he heaved a sigh.

"Sigh of a king's son under spells!" said the horse. "Mount, and you shall get the silver cup. The people of Norroway are gathered about the king tonight, for he has missed his daughter, and when you get to the palace go in and leave me without; they will have the cup there going round the company. Go in and sit in their midst. Say nothing, and seem to be as one of the people of the place. But when the cup comes round to you, tuck it under your arm, and come out to me with it, and we'll go."

Away they went and they got to Norroway, and the king's son went in to the palace and did as the black horse bade. He took the cup and came out and mounted, and before sunrise he was in the Land Underwaves.

"You are come," said the prince.

"I am come," said he.

"We had better get married now," said the prince to the princess.

"Slowly and softly," said she. "I will not marry till I get the silver ring that my grandmother and my mother wore when they were wedded."

"You, rider of the black horse," said the prince, "do that. Let's have that ring here tomorrow at sunrise."

The king's son went to the black horse and put his elbow on his crest and told him how it was.

"There never was a matter set before me harder than this matter that has now been set before me," said the horse, "but there is no help for it at any rate. Get up on me. There is a snow mountain and an ice mountain and a mountain of fire between us and the winning of that ring. It is right hard for us to pass them."

Thus they went as they were, and about a mile from the snow mountain they were in a bad case with cold. As they came near it the king's son struck the horse, and with the bound he gave the black horse was on the top of the snow mountain; at the next bound he was on the top of the ice mountain; at the third bound he went through the mountain of fire. When he had passed the mountains the king's son was dragging at the horse's neck, as though he were about to lose himself. He went on before him down to a town below.

"Go down," said the black horse, "to a smithy; make an iron spike for every bone end in me."

Down he went as the horse desired, and he got the spikes made, and back he came with them.

"Stick them into me," said the horse, "every spike of them in every bone end that I have."

That he did; he stuck the spikes into the horse.

"There is a loch here," said the horse, "four miles long and four miles wide, and when I go into it the loch will take fire and blaze. If you see the Loch of Fire going out before the sun rises, expect me; and if not, go your way."

Out went the black horse into the lake, and the lake became flame. Long was he stretched about the lake, beating his palms and roaring, the king's son. Day came, and the lake did not go out.

But at the hour when the sun was rising from the water the lake went out.

And the black horse rose in the middle of the water with one single spike in him, and the ring upon its end.

He came on shore, and down he fell beside the lake.

Then down went the rider. He got the ring, and he dragged the horse down to the side of a hill. He fell to sheltering him with his arms about him, and as the sun was rising he got better and better, till about midday, when he stood on his feet.

"Get up," said the horse, "and let us be gone."

He got up on the black horse, and away they went.

He reached the mountains, and he leaped the horse at the fire mountain and was on the top. From the mountain of fire he leaped to the mountain of ice, and from the mountain of ice to the mountain of snow. He put the mountains past him, and by morning he was in the Land Underwaves.

"You are come," said the prince.

"I am," said he.

"That's true," said the prince. "A king's son are you, but a son of success am I. We shall have no more mistakes and delays, but a wedding this time."

"Go easy," said the princess of Norroway. "Your wedding is not so near as you think yet. Till you make a castle, I won't marry you. Not to your father's castle nor to your mother's castle will I go to dwell; but make me a castle for which your father's castle would not make washing water."

"You, rider of the black horse, make that," said the prince, "before the morrow's sun rises."

The lad went out to the horse and leaned his elbow on his neck and sighed, thinking that this castle never could be made for ever.

"There never came a turn in my road yet that is easier for me to pass than this," said the black horse.

The king's son gave a glance, and he saw ever so many wrights and stone masons at work, and the castle was ready before the sun rose.

He shouted at the prince of the Land Underwaves, and he saw the castle. He tried to pluck out his eye, thinking that it was a false sight.

"Prince," said the rider of the black horse, "don't think that you have a false sight; this is a true sight."

"That may be," said the prince. "You are a son of success, but I am a son of success, too. There will be no more mistakes and delays, but a wedding now."

"No," said the princess. "Should we not go to look at the castle? There's time enough to get married before the night comes."

They went to the castle and the castle was without want.

"I see one," said the prince. "One want at least to be made good. A well to be made inside, so that water may not be far to fetch when there is a feast or a wedding in the castle."

"That won't be long undone," said the rider of the black horse.

The well was made, and it was seven fathoms deep and two or three fathoms wide, and they looked at the well on the way to the wedding.

"It is fairly made," said the princess, "but for one fault yonder."

"Where is it?" said the prince.

"There," said she.

He bent him down to look. She came out, and she put her two hands at his back, and cast him in.

"Be thou there," said she. "If I go to be married, thou art not the man; but the man who did each thing that has been done, and, if he chooses, him will I have."

Away she went with the rider of the little black horse to the wedding.

And at the end of three years after that so it was that the king's son first remembered the black horse or where he left him.

He got up and went out, and he was very sorry for his neglect of the black horse. He found him just where he had left him at the wedding.

"Good luck to you, gentleman," said the horse. "You seem as if you had got something that you like better than me."

"I have not got that, and I won't; but it came over me to forget you," said he.

"I don't mind," said the horse, "it will make no difference. Raise your sword and smite off my head."

"Fortune will not allow that I should do that," said he.

"Do it at once, or I will do it to you," said the horse.

So the lad drew his sword and smote off the horse's head; then he lifted his two palms and uttered a doleful cry.

What should he hear behind him but, "All hail, my brother-in-law."

He looked behind him, and there was the finest man he ever set eyes upon.

"What set you weeping for the black horse?" said the fine man.

"This," said the king's son: "that there never was born of man or beast a creature in this world that I was fonder of."

"Would you take me for him?" said the stranger.

"If I could think you the horse, I would; but if not, I would rather the horse," said the rider.

"I am the black horse," said he. "And if I were not, how should you have all these things that you went to seek in my father's house? Since I went under spells, many a man have I ran at before you met me. They had but one word amongst them: they could not keep me nor manage me, and they never kept me a couple of days. But when I fell in with you, you kept me till the time ran out that was to come from the spells. And now you shall go home with me, and we shall make a wedding in my father's house."

GOLD·TREE and SILVER·TREE

nce upon a time there was a king and he had a wife; her name was Silver-Tree. He had a daughter; her name was Gold-Tree.

On a day of days, Gold-Tree and Silver-Tree went to a glen, where there was a spring, and in the spring there was a trout.

Said Silver-Tree, "Troutie, bonny fellow, am not I the most beautiful queen in the world?"

"Indeed you are not," said the trout.

"Who then?" said Silver-Tree.

"Why, Gold-Tree, your daughter," said the trout.

Silver-Tree went home. She lay down on her bed, and vowed she would never be well until she could get the heart and the liver of Gold-Tree, her daughter, to eat.

At nightfall the king came home, and it was told to him that Silver-Tree, his wife, was ill. He went where she was, and asked her what was wrong with her.

"Oh," said Silver-Tree, "only a thing that you may heal if you like."

"Oh," said the king, "there is nothing at all that I could do for you that I would not do."

Said Silver-Tree, "If I get the heart and the liver of Gold-Tree, my daughter, to eat, I shall be well."

Now it happened about this time that the son of a great king had come to ask Gold-Tree for marrying. The king now agreed to this, and they went away secretly.

The king then went and sent his lads to the hunting hill for a he-goat, and he gave its heart and its liver to his wife to eat; and she rose up well and healthy.

A year after this Silver-Tree went to the glen, where there was the spring in which there was the trout.

She said, "Troutie, bonny fellow, am I not the most beautiful queen in the world?"

"Indeed you are not."

"Who then?"

"Why, Gold-Tree, your daughter."

"Oh well, it is long since she was living."

"Oh indeed she is not dead. She is married to a prince over the waves."

Silver-Tree went home, and begged the king to put the ship in order, and said, "I am going to see my dear Gold-Tree, for it is long since I saw her." The ship was put in order, and she went away. It was Silver-Tree herself that was at the helm, and she steered the ship so true that she was not long at all before she came to the country of the prince over the waves.

The prince was out hunting on the hills. Gold-Tree knew the ship of her father coming.

"Oh!" she said to the servants, "My mother is here, and she will kill me."

"She shall not kill you at all," they said. "We shall lock you in a room where she cannot get near you."

This is how it was done; and when Silver-Tree came ashore, she began to cry out, "Come to meet your own mother, when she comes to see you!" Gold-Tree said that she could not, that she was locked in the room, and that she could not get out.

"Will you not put out," said Silver-Tree, "your little finger through the keyhole, so that your own mother may give a kiss to it?"

Gold-Tree put out her little finger, and Silver-Tree went and put a poisoned stab in it, and Gold-Tree fell dead.

When the prince came home, and found Gold-Tree dead, he was in great sorrow, and when he saw how beautiful she was, he did not bury her at all, but he locked her in a room where nobody would get near her.

The prince married again, and the whole house was under the hand of this wife but one room, and he himself always kept the key of it. On a day of days he forgot to take the key with him, and the second wife got into the room. What did she see there but the most beautiful woman that she ever saw.

The wife began to turn and try to wake her, and she noticed the poison stab in her finger. She took the stab out, and Gold-Tree rose alive, as fair as she ever was.

At night the prince came home with an ill look on his face. "What gift," said his wife, "would you give me that I could make you laugh?"

"Oh indeed," said the prince, "nothing could make me laugh, except Gold-Tree were to come alive again."

"Well," said his wife, "you will find her alive down there in the room."

When the prince saw Gold-Tree alive he made great rejoicings, and he began to kiss her, and kiss her, and kiss her. Said the second wife, "Since she is the first one you had, it is better for you to stick to her, and I shall go away."

"Oh indeed," said the prince, "you shall not go away, but I shall have both of you."

At the end of a year, Silver-Tree went to the glen, where there was the spring, in which there was the trout.

"Troutie, bonny fellow, am I not the most beautiful queen in the world?"

"Indeed you are not."

"Who then?"

"Why, Gold-Tree, your daughter."

"Oh well, she is not alive. It is a year since I put the poisoned stab into her finger."

"Oh indeed she is not dead at all, at all."

Silver-Tree went home, and begged the king to put the ship in order, for that she was going to see her dear Gold-Tree, as it was so long since she saw her. The ship was put in order, and she went away. It was Silver-Tree herself that was at the helm, and she steered the ship so well that she was not long before she came to that country.

The prince was out hunting on the hills. Gold-Tree knew her father's ship coming.

"Oh!" said she, "My mother is coming, and she will kill me."

"Not at all," said the second wife. "We shall go down to meet her."

Silver-Tree came ashore. "Come down, Gold-Tree, love," said she, "for your own mother has come to you with a drink."

"It is custom in this country," said the second wife, "that the one who offers a drink takes a draught out of it first."

Silver-Tree put her mouth to the drink, and the second wife went and struck it so that the drink went down her throat, and she fell dead. They had only to carry her home a corpse and bury her.

The prince and his two wives were long alive after this, pleased and peaceful.

THE FLYING CHILDER

’m scarce sure if I can tell you it all right, but I guess I mind it as it was told to me. Let's see, now.

There was once a chap as was great for the womenfolk, and couldn't keep out of their way if he tried ever so. The very sight of a petticoat half a mile off on the road would call him for to follow it.

Now one day, as it might be, he came ker-bang round a corner, and there was the rampingest maid, sitting her lone, and washing herself; and the fond chap was all out of his wits to want. And the upshot of it was, he swore he would wed her if she would come home with him. And she said: "I'll come, and welcome," says she, "but you must swear as you'll wed me."

"I will," says he. "I swear it." – and thought to himself, "Over the left shoulder, that!"

"You must wed me in church," says she.

"I will," says he. "If ever I put foot in," he thought to himself.

"And if you don't, what shall I forspell you?" says she.

"Lawks," says he, for he was feared of being forspelled, which is main mischancy, you see; "don't you overlook me, don't you! If I don't wed you, may the worms eat me," – ("They're bound for to do it, anyway," thinks he to himself) – "and the childer have wings and fly away." ("And no great matter if they do," thinks he.)

But the maid didn't know what he was thinking, and she went with him. And by and by they came to a church.

"You can wed me here-by," says she, tweaking his arm.

"No," says he, "the parson's a-hunting."

So they went on a bit further, and came to another church.

"Well, here-by?" says she.

"No," says he. "Parson's none sober enough, and the clerk's drunk."

"Well!" says she. "May be they will can wed us, for all they're in liquor."

"Houts!" says he, and gives her a kick.

So on they went again, and by and by they met with a tailor-man, and he says, says he, to the tailor-man: "Where's your master?"

"Oh, down-by," says he.

So on they went, till they came to a bit cottage by the lane side, and they knocked and kicked at the door till it shook, but never a word came from innard. So they walked right in, and there was an old man lying sleeping and snoring on his bed.

Well, the young chap keckt about him for summat handy, and saw an axe; so he upped with it and brained the old feller, and chopped his feet and hands off him. And then he set to and cleaned the place, and thrung the corp out of the window, and laid the fire in the hearth, while all was smart and natty.

Then they lived there, him and the girl, and had some childer.

And by and by, kecking over his shoulder, the chap saw a wise woman stealing the corp away with her.

"Hi!" says the chap. "The corp is mine. What do you want to do with him?"

"I'll bury him for you," says the wise woman.

"No you won't," says he. "I'll do it myself."

"Well then," says she, "I'll stand by."

"No you won't," says he. "I can do it better my lone."

"Take your way, fool," says she, "but give me the axe, then, instead of the corp."

"No I won't," says he. "I might want her again."

"Hi!" says the wise woman. "None have, none give; red hand and lying lips!"

And she went away, muttering, and twisting her fingers.

So the chap buried the corp; but lest he forgot where it was, he left one arm sticking out of the ground; and the feet and hands he chucked to the pigs; and says he to the girl: "I'll go and snare a cony. See you keep to the house." And off he went.

The girl diddle-daddled about, and presently the pigs began squealing as if they were killed.

"And oh!" says the girl, "what's amiss with them for so to squeal?"

And the dead feet upped and cried, "We be amiss. Us'll trample the pigs till you bury us!"

So she took the feet and put them in the earth.

And by and by the pigs lay down and died.

"Oh! Oh!" says the girl. "What be the matter with them for so to die?"

And the dead hands upped and cried, "We be the matter. We's choked them!"

So she went and buried the hands, too.

And by and by she heard summat a-calling, and a-calling on her, and she went for to see what it wanted.

"Who be a-calling?" says she.

"You've put us wrong!" says the feet and hands. "We be feeling, and we be creeping, and we can't find the rest of us anywheres. Put us by the old man, where his arm sticks out of the ground, or we'll tickle you with fingers and tread you with toes, till you lose your wits."

So she dug them up, and put them by the old man.

And by and by the young chap came back, and called for his dinner.

"Where's the childer?" says he.

"Gathering berries," says she.

"Berries in spring?" says he; and kept on with his eating. But when night came, and they weren't home: "Where's the childer?" says he.

"Gone a-fishing," says she.

"Ay," says he, "and the babby, too?"

And came the morning, he shook the girl up sudden, and bawled in her ears: "Where's the childer?"

"Ooh!" says she in a hurry, "flown away, the childer have!"

"They have?" says he. "Then you will can go after them!"

And he upped with the axe and chopped her in pieces, and shoved the bits under the bed.

Well by and by the childer came flying back, and keckt about for their mother, but they saw nowt.

"Where's mother?" they say to the chap.

"Gone to buy bacon," says he, feeling uneasy.

"Bacon?" says they. "And with flitches hanging ready?"

And presently they came again, and says: "Where's mother now?"

"Gone to seek you," says he, shaking under the bedclothes.

"Ay?" says they. "And we be here!"

And before he could get out of bed they came all round him, and pointed at him with their fingers.

"Where's mother to-now?"

"Ooh!" he squealed. "Under the bed!" And he put his head under the blanket.

The children pulled out the bits, and fell to weeping and wailing as they pieced her together. And the chap, he went for to creep to the door and get away, but they caught him, and took the axe and chopped him up like the girl, and left him lying whiles they went away, gratting.

As soon as he was sure he was dead, the chap got up and shook himself – and there was the girl! She was standing waiting for him, with long claws out, and teeth gibbering, and eyes blazing like a green cat going to spring. And naturally the chap was feared, and he runned, and runned, and runned, so as to get away; but she runned after, with her long claws straight out, till he could feel her tickling the back of his neck, and straining with the longing to choke him. And he called out to the thunder: "Strike me dead!"

But the thunder wouldn't, for he was dead already.

And he runned to the fire and begged: "Burn me up!"

But the fire wouldn't, for the chill of death put it out.

And he thrung himself into the water and says: "Drown me blue!"

But the water wouldn't, for the death-colour was coming in his face already.

And he took the axe and tried to cut his throat, but the axe wouldn't.

And to last, he thrung himself into the ground, and called for the worms to eat him, so as he could rest in his grave and be quit of the woman.

But by and by up crept a great worm, and a strange and great thing it was, with the girl's head on the end of its long slimy body, and it crept up beside him and round about, and over him, while it drove away all the other worms, and then it set to, to eat him himself.

"Ooh, eat me quick, eat me quick!" he squeals.

"Steady now," says the worm. "Good food's worth the meal time. You hold still, and let me enjoy myself."

"Eat me quick, eat me quick!" says he.

"Don't you haste me, I tell you," says the worm. "I's getting on fine. You're near gone now." And it smacked its lips with the goodness of it.

"Quick!" he whispit again.

"Whist, you're an unpatient chap," said the worm.

And it swallowed the last bit, and the lad was all gone, and had got away from the girl to last.

And that's all.

The Castle of Melvales

nce upon a time there was an old king, who had three sons. And the old king fell very sick one time, and there was nothing at all could make him well but some golden apples from a far country. So the three brothers went on horseback to look for some of those apples to recover their father.

The three brothers set off together; and when they come to some cross-roads, they halted and refreshed themselves a bit. And there they agreed to meet on a certain time, and not one was to go home before the other. So Valentine took the right, and Oliver went on straight, and poor Jack took the left. And, so as to make my long story short, I shall follow poor Jack, and leave the other two to take their chance, for I don't think there was much good in them.

Well now, poor Jack rides off over hills, dales, valleys, and mountains, through woolly woods and sheepwalks, where the old chap never sounded his hollow bugle horn, further than I can tell you tonight, or ever I intend to tell you.

At last he came to some old house near a great forest, and there was some old man sitting out by the door; ugly, he was. The old man said to him, "Good morning, my king's son."

"Good morning to you, old gentleman," was the answer by Jack, and frightened out of his wits, but he did not like to give in.

The old gentleman told him to dismount and to go in and have some refreshment, and to put his horse in the stable, such as it was. And Jack, after going in, and having something to eat, and after his long ride, he began to ask the old man how did he know that he was a king's son.

"Oh dear!" said the old man, "I knew that you was a king's son, and I knew what is your business better than what you do yourself. So you will have to stay here tonight; and when you are in bed, you mustn't be frightened when you hear something come to you. There will come all manner of snakes and frogs, and some will try to get into your eyes and into your mouth. And mind," the old man said, "if you stir the least bit, then you will turn into one of those things yourself."

Poor Jack did not know what to make of this, but however, he ventured to go to bed; and just as he thought to have a bit of sleep, here they came around him, but he never stirred one bit all night.

"Well, my young son, how are you this morning?"

"Oh! I am very well, thank you, but I did not have much rest."

"Well, never mind that. You have got on so far, but you have a great deal to go through before you can have the golden apples to fetch to your father. So now you better come to have some breakfast before you start on your way to my other brother's house. Now you will have to leave your own horse here with me, until you come back here again to me, and to tell me everything about how you got on."

After that, out comes a fresh horse for Jack. And the old man give him a ball of yarn; and he flung it between the horse's two ears. And off he goes as fast as the wind, which the wind behind could not catch the wind before, until he came to the second oldest brother's house.

When he rode up to the door, he had the same salute as he had from the first old man; but this one was much uglier than the first. He had long grey hair, and his teeth were curling out of his mouth, and his finger and toe nails were not cut for many thousands of years; so I shall leave you to guess what sort of a looking being he was.

The old man puts the horse in a much better stable, and calls Jack in, and gives him plenty to eat and drink, and lots of tobacco and brandy; and they have a bit of chat before they goes to bed.

"Well, my young son, I suppose that you are one of the king's sons, and come to look for the golden apples to recover him because he is sick."

"Yes; I am the youngest of the brothers, and I should like well to get them to go back with."

"Well, don't mind, my young son. I will send word before you tonight to my oldest brother, when you go to bed, and I will say all to him what you want, and then he will not have much trouble to send you on to the place where you must go to get them. But you must mind tonight not to stir when you hear those things biting and stinging you, or else you will work great mischief to yourself."

Jack went to bed, and bore all, as he did the first night, and got up the next morning well and hearty. After a good breakfast he said what a curious place that was, and the old man said, "Yes; but you will see a more curious place soon; and I hope I shall see you back here all right."

Then out comes another fresh horse, and a ball of yarn to throw between its ears. The old man tells Jack to jump up, and says to him that he has made it all right with his oldest brother to give him a quick reception, and not to delay any whatever, as he has a good deal to go through in a very short and quick time.

Jack flung the ball, and off he goes as quick as lightning, and comes to the oldest brother's house. Well, to make my long story short, this one was the ugliest yet, and he received Jack very kindly, and told him that he long wished to see him, and that he would go through his work like a man, and return back here safe and sound.

"Now tonight," he said, "I shall give you rest; there shall nothing come to disturb you. And you must mind to get up middling early, for you've got to go and come all in the same day. There will be no place for you to rest within thousands of miles; and if there was, you would stand in danger never to come from there in your own form. Now mind what I tell you.

"Tomorrow, when you go in sight of a very large castle, which will be surrounded with black water, the first thing you will do you will tie your horse to a tree, and you will see three beautiful swans in sight. Then you will say, 'Swan, swan, carry me over, for the name of the Griffin of the Greenwood'; and the swans will swim you over to the castle.

"There will be three great entrances, before you go in. The first will be guarded by four great giants, and drawn swords in their hands; the second entrance, five great cats; and the third, six great fiery serpents, too frightful to mention. You will have to be there exactly at one o'clock; and mind and leave there exactly at two, and not a moment later.

"When you pass all these things, when the swans carry you over, all will be fast asleep, but you must not notice any one of them. When you go in, you will turn up to the right, you will see some grand rooms, then you will go downstairs and through the cooking kitchen, and through a door on your left you go into a garden, where you will find the apples you want for your father to get him well.

"After you fill your wallet, you make all the speed you possibly can, and call out for the swans to carry you over the same as they did before. And after you get on your horse, should you hear any shouting or making any noise after you, be sure not to look back, as they will follow you for thousands of miles; but when the time will be up and you near my place, it will be all over.

"Well, now, Jack, I have told you all you have to do tomorrow; and mind, whatever you do, never look about you when you see all those dreadful things. Keep a good heart, and make haste from there, and come back to me with all the speed you can. And now let's take a drop more brandy and a little tobacco, and then let's go to bed. There are no snakes here."

Jack went to bed, and had a good night's rest, and got up the next morning as fresh as a newly caught trout. After breakfast, out comes a horse, and, when saddling and fettling, the old man begins to laugh and tells Jack that if he sees a pretty young lady, not to stay with her too long, because she may waken, and then he would have to stay with her, or to be turned into one of those monsters like those he will have to pass by going into the castle.

"I think I shall come out all right," says Jack, "if I sees a young lady there, you may depend."

So Jack mounts his horse, and off he goes like a shot out of a gun. At last he comes in sight of the castle. He ties his horse safe to a tree, and, at a quarter to one, he calls out, "Swan, swan, carry me over, for the name of the Griffin of the Greenwood."

No sooner said than done. A swan under each side, and one in front, took him over in a crack. He got on his legs, and walked quietly by all those four great giants, five great cats and six fiery serpents too frightful to mention, while they were all asleep, and that only for the space of one hour, then into the castle he goes, neck or nothing.

He turns to the right, upstairs he runs, and enters into a very grand room, and sees a beautiful princess lying full stretch on a beautiful gold bedstead, fast asleep.

Jack gazed on her beautiful form with admiration, and looked at her foot, and said, "Where there is a pretty foot, there must be a pretty leg." And he takes her garter off, and buckles it on his own leg, and he buckles his on hers; and he takes her gold watch and pocket-handkerchief, and he exchanges his for hers; and after that ventures to give her a kiss, when she very near opened her eyes.

Seeing the time short, off Jack runs downstairs, through the cooking kitchen to go into the garden for the apples, and he sees the cook all-fours on her back in the middle of the floor, with the knife in one hand and the fork in the other. He found the apples out, and filled his wallet well; and by his passing through the kitchen again the cook did very near waken, and she did wink on him with one eye.

Jack called out for the swans, and off they managed to take him over, for the name of the Griffin of the Greenwood, but they found he was a sight heavier than when he was going before.

No sooner than he had mounted his horse, he could hear a tremendous noise, and the enchantment was broke, and they tried to follow him, but all to no purpose. He was not long before he came to the oldest brother's house; and glad enough he was to see it, for the sight and the noise of all those things that were after him near frightened him to death.

The old man said, "Welcome, Jack, I am proud to see you. Dismount and put the horse in the stable, and come in and have some refreshment. I know you are hungry after all you have gone through in that castle. And tell all what you did, and all what you saw there. There was other kings' sons went by here to go to that castle, but they never came back alive. And now you must come with me, and a sword in your hand, and must cut my head off and must throw it in that well."

Jack put the horse in the stable, and then went in to have some refreshment, for he wanted some. And after telling everything that had passed, which the old man was very pleased to hear, they both went for a walk together, the place all around looking dreadful. The old man could scarcely walk from his toe nails curling up like rams' horns that had not been cut for many hundred years, and big long hair, and the teeth looping out of his mouth. They come to a well, and he gives the lad a sword, and tells him to cut his head off and throw it down that well. Jack has to do it against his wish, but he has to do it.

No sooner he does it, and flings the head in the well, than up springs one of the finest young gentlemen you would wish to see; and instead of the old house and the frightful place, it was changed into a beautiful hall and garden.

And they went back, and enjoyed themselves well, and had a good laugh about the castle, especially when Jack told him about the cook winking on him and could not open the other eye. Jack leaves this young gentleman in all his glory, and he tells Jack that he will see him again before long. They have a jolly shake-hands, and off Jack goes to the next oldest brother, and has to serve him, to cut off his head, and all turned out as it had with the first; then away he went to the youngest brother, who began asking him how things went on, and making inquiries and saying, "Did you see my two brothers?"

"Yes," said Jack.

"How did they look?" said he.

"They looked very well. I liked them much. They told me many things what to do."

"Well, did you go to the castle?"

"Well, I did."

"And will you tell me what you saw in there? Did you see the young lady?"

152

"Yes, I saw her, and plenty other frightful things."

"Did you hear any snakes biting you in my oldest brother's bed?"

"No, there were none there; I slept well."

"You won't have to sleep in the same bed tonight. You will have to cut off my head in the morning."

Jack had a good night's rest, and changed all the appearance of the place by cutting the head off before he started in the morning. He had a good breakfast, and took for himself a little brandy and a good lot of tobacco for the road. There was a jolly shake-hands, and the young man tells Jack it's very probable that he shall see him again soon. His house was pretty, and the country around it beautiful, after having his head cut off.

Away Jack goes, near losing the apples with his rough riding, and he comes to the cross-roads where he has to meet his two brothers on the very day appointed.

He sees no tracks of horses, and, being tired, he lays himself down to sleep, ties the horse to his leg, and puts the apples under his head.

Presently up come the other brothers, the same time to the minute, and found Jack fast asleep. And they would not waken him, but said one to another, "Let's see what sort of apples he has got under his head." So they took and tasted them, and found they were different from theirs. They took and changed his apples for theirs, and hooked it off to London as fast as they could, and left the poor lad sleeping.

After a while Jack awoke, and, seeing the tracks of other horses, he mounted and off with him, not thinking about the apples being changed.

He had still a long way to go by himself, and by the time he got near London he could hear all the bells in the town ringing, but he did not know what was the matter until he rode up to the palace, when he found that his father was recovered by his brothers' apples, and they had gone off to some sport for a while.

The king was very glad to see his youngest son, and was anxious to taste his apples; but when he found that they were not good, and thought that they were more for poisoning him, he sent immediately for the butcher to behead his youngest son.

Jack was taken away there and then in a carriage; but instead of the butcher chopping his head off, he took him to some forest not far from the town, because he had pity on him, and there left him to take his chance. When presently up comes a big hairy bear, limping upon three legs; and Jack, poor lad, climbed up a tree, frightened of him, and the bear told him to come down, that it's no use of him to stop there. The bear said, "Come here to me. I will not do you any harm. I know you are hungry all this time."

With hard persuasion Jack comes down, and he did not see that he snagged the gold watch on a twig and left it there, the watch he had changed with the princess asleep in the castle.

Jack said, "No, I am not very hungry; but I was very frightened when I saw you coming first, when I had no place to run away from you."

The bear said, "I was also afraid of you, when I saw that butcher setting you down from that carriage. I thought you would not mind killing me if you would see me. But when I saw the butcher going away and leaving you behind by yourself, I made bold to come to you, and now I know who you are very well. Aren't you the king's youngest son? I've seen you and your brothers and lots of other gentlemen in this wood many times. Now, before we go from here, I must tell you that I am a Gypsy in disguise; and I shall take you where we are stopping at."

Young Jack ups and tells the bear everything from first to last, how he started in search of the apples, and about the three old men, and about the castle, and how he was served at last by his father after he came home, and instead of the butcher to take his head off, he was kind enough to leave him to have his life, and to take his chance in the forest, live or die. "And here I am now, under your protection," says Jack.

The bear tells him, "Come on, my brother. There shall be no harm to you as long as you are with me."

So he takes Jack up to the tents, and when they see them coming, the girls begin to laugh, and say, "Here is our Jubal coming with a young gentleman."

When he advanced nearer the tents, they all began to know that he was the young prince that had passed by that way many times before; and when Jubal went to change himself, he called most of them together in one tent, and told them everything all about him, and told them to be kind to him. And so they were, for there was nothing he desired but what he had, the same as if he was in the palace with his father and mother. He was let to romp and play with the girls, but no further, and he had lessons on the Welsh harp.

Jubal, after he pulled off his hairy coat, was one of the smartest young men, and he stuck to be Jack's closest companion. Jack was always sociable and merry, except he would think of his gold watch. The butcher had allowed him to keep that for company, and did not like to take it from him, as it might come useful to him some time or other. And the poor lad did not know where he lost it, being so much excited with everything.

Jack passed off many happy days in Epping Forest with the Woods and the Roberts, who were Welsh Gypsies out of North Wales, and with the Stanleys and Greys, too. But one day Jack and poor Jubal were strolling through the trees, when they came to the very same spot where they first met, and, accidentally looking up, Jack could see his watch hanging in the tree that he had to climb when he first saw Jubal coming to him in the form of a bear; and he cries out, "Jubal! Jubal! I can see my watch up in that tree!"

"Well! I am sure, how lucky!" said Jubal. "Shall I go and get it down?"

"No, I'd rather go myself," said Jack.

Now when all this was going on, the young princess whom Jack changed those things with in that castle, seeing that one of the King of England's sons had been there by the changing of the watch, and other things, got herself ready with a large army, and sailed off for England.

She left her army a little out of the town; and she took her fine young boy with her and she went with her guards straight up to the palace to see the king, and also demanded to see his sons.

They had a long talk together about this and that; and at last she demands one of the sons to come before her; and the oldest comes, and she asks him, "Have you ever been at the Castle of Melvales?" And he answers, "Yes."

She throws down a pocket-handkerchief, bids him to walk over that without stumbling. He goes to walk over it, and no sooner he put his foot on it he fell down and broke his leg. He was taken off right away and made a prisoner of by his own guards. The other brother was called upon, and was asked the same question, "Have you ever been at the Castle of Melvales?", and he had to go through the same performance, and he broke his leg and was made a prisoner of.

Now the princess says, "Have you not another son?"

The king began to shiver and shake and knock his two knees together that he could scarcely stand upon his legs, and did not know what to say to her; he was so much frightened. At last a thought came to him to send for his butcher, and inquired of him particularly, "Did you behead my son, or is he alive?"

"He is saved, O King."

"Then bring him here at once, or else I shall be done for."

Two of the fastest horses they had were put in the carriage, to go and look for the poor Welsh-harping prince in Epping Forest. And when they got to the very self same spot where they left him, that was the time when Jack was up the tree getting his watch down, and Jubal standing a distance off.

They called out to Jubal, "Did you see another young man in this wood?"

Jubal thought something, and did not like to say No, and said Yes, and pointed up the tree. And they told Jack to come down at once, as there was a young lady in search of him with a young child.

"Jubal," says Jack, "did you ever hear such a thing in all your life, my brother?"

"Do you call him your brother?" says they.

"Well, he has been better to me than my brothers."

"Well, for his kindness he shall come with you to the palace, and see how things will turn out."

After they go to the palace, Jack has a good wash, and appears before the princess, when she puts the question to him, "Have you ever been at the Castle of Melvales?" And he gave a graceful bow.

And says my lady, "Walk over that handkerchief without stumbling."

He walked over it many times, and danced upon it, and nothing happened to him.

The princess said, with a proud and smiling air, "That is the young man"; and out come the exchanged things by both of them. She ordered a big box to be brought in and to be opened, and she took out some of the most costly uniforms that were ever on an emperor's back; and when Jack dressed himself up, the king could scarcely look upon him for the dazzling of the gold and diamonds on his coat and that.

Jack ordered his two brothers to be in prison for a time; and before the princess demanded him to go with her to her own country, she went visiting to Jubal's camp, and she made them all some handsome presents for being so kind to young Jack. She gave Jubal an invitation to go with them, wished them a hearty farewell for a while, promising to meet them by saying, "Cheer up, mates. I shall see you in my country by and by."

They went back to the king to bid him not to be so hasty in future to order peoples' heads off before having proper cause. Then away they marched, and all their army with them. But while the soldiers were striking their tents, Jack bethought himself of his Welsh harp, and had it fetched from Epping to take with him in a beautiful wooden case.

After they crossed over, they called to visit each of the three brothers Jack had to stay with on his way to the Castle of Melvales; and a merry time they had of it, when they all got together.

The Castle of Melvales

And now I've come to the finish. The last time I seen him, I played upon Jack's harp; and he told me he should like to see me in North Wales again another day.

"That's my story, and if there's a lie
in it, let there be. 'Tis long ago I
heard it from my father. He had the
world of stories. I had a lot of them,
but alas, my memory is gone and my mind
is astray now, and I can't help that."

Peig Sayers: *storyteller*.

(1873–1958)

SOURCES

Tom Tit Tot Adapted from E. S. Hartland: County Folk-Lore I, Gloucestershire: London: 1892.

Jack and the Green Lady Adapted from *The Grey Castle*: "A Book of Gypsy Folk Tales": Dora E. Yates: J. M. Dent & Sons Ltd: London: 1948.

Mally Whuppy Adapted from "Popular Tales of the West Highlands": J. F. Campbell: London: 1890/3.

Yallery Brown Adapted from "Legends of the Lincolnshire Cars": M. C. Balfour: Folklore II: 1891.

The Black Bull of Norroway Adapted from "Popular Rhymes of Scotland": R. Chambers: Edinburgh: 1890.

Mossycoat Adapted from "A Dictionary of British Folk-Tales": Katharine M. Briggs: Routledge & Kegan Paul plc: London: 1970.

Kate Crackernuts Adapted from D. J. Robinson: Folklore I: 1890.

The Battle of the Birds Adapted from J. F. Campbell.

The Green Mist Adapted from M. C. Balfour.

The Rose Tree Adapted from "Folklore of the Northern Counties of England": W. Henderson: London: 1866.

The Little Fox Adapted from "Gypsy Folk-Tales": F. H. Groome: London: 1899.

The Old Witch Adapted from "More English Fairy Tales": J. Jacobs: London: 1894.

The Seawife and the Crone Adapted from J. F. Campbell.

The Little Bull Calf Adapted from F. H. Groome.

Mr. Fox Adapted from "English Fairy Tales": J. Jacobs: London: 1890.

The Paddo Adapted from R. Chambers.

The Golden Ball Adapted from W. Henderson.

The Black Horse Adapted from "More Celtic Fairy Tales": J. Jacobs: London: 1894.

Gold-Tree and Silver-Tree Adapted from Celtic Magazine XIII: n.d.

The Flying Childer Adapted from M. C. Balfour.

The Castle of Melvales Adapted from F. H. Groome.